Prophetic Statesmanship

Prophetic Statesmanship

Harry Jaffa, Abraham Lincoln, and the Gettysburg Address

Edward J. Erler

New York • London

Encounter
BOOKS

First American edition published in 2025 by Encounter Books,
an activity of Encounter for Culture and Education, Inc.,
a nonprofit, tax exempt corporation.
Encounter Books website address: www.encounterbooks.com

Manufactured in Canada and printed on
acid-free paper. The paper used in this publication meets
the minimum requirements of ANSI/NISO Z39.48–1992 (R 1997)
(*Permanence of Paper*).

FIRST AMERICAN EDITION

LIBRARY OF CONGRESS CATALOGING-IN-PUBLICATION DATA IS
AVAILABLE

Information for this title can be found at the Library of Congress
website under the following
ISBN 978-1-64177-461-1 and LCCN 2025005052.

CONTENTS

*This book is dedicated
to the good students of
Harry Victor Jaffa.*

INTRODUCTION

"Natural right is a part of political right and has everywhere the same force or power (δύναμιν) but is everywhere changeable."

—ARISTOTLE—

It has fallen to my lot at the request of Harry V. Jaffa to complete *A New Birth of Freedom*, which was originally planned, not only as "the sequel to *Crisis of the House Divided*," but a sustained "commentary on the Gettysburg Address." Chapter two of *A New Birth* is entitled "The Declaration of Independence, the Gettysburg Address, and the Historians," yet scarcely more than two and a half pages of the chapter's seventy-nine pages are dedicated to the speech that the chapter title promises to be the central topic. Jaffa seems to have been more interested at this juncture in Lincoln's deeper and more fundamental statement of America's "dedication to the proposition that all men are created equal" than he was in the speech itself. *A New Birth of Freedom* is a sustained commentary on this "proposition." This is why Jaffa thought a second volume was required to complete the task—a commentary on the Gettysburg Address.

Am I the one to do it? I certainly do not have the comprehensive knowledge that Jaffa brought to the task, nor do I possess the lively writing skills he exhibited. I say nothing of

1

Jaffa's considerable rhetorical skills. But I am not entirely disarmed! The burden Jaffa placed on me is great. If he thought I could shoulder that burden, then I am obliged to try.

I was close to Harry Jaffa in his last years and saw him frequently. We spoke about many things, but mainly of the topics that preoccupied him during what he called his "summing up," Plato and Shakespeare. I asked him several times if I could record his musings, but he always refused with undisguised contempt, saying "just listen and think with me." Always good advice and advice I had frequently given my students. Coming from Harry Jaffa this was a special charge and a heavy one that I was not certain I could bear, but it was one that was a great benefit to me, and Jaffa knew it would be.

On one occasion I arrived early in the afternoon to find Jaffa in an agitated and disconsolate mood. "What's wrong, Harry," I asked, not a little concerned. "I was just thinking," he said, "what a tragedy it is that Socrates never had a chance to read Shakespeare's *Hamlet*. He is the only one who could have understood the psychological depth and complexities of the play." I was tempted to reply, "Why *Hamlet*?", but I didn't, knowing it was my obligation to think it through. His next reflection, which came in rapid sequence was "I have been thinking about the connection between *Hamlet* and *Macbeth* and how those two plays are essential for understating Shakespeare." Again, I didn't dare respond, but I now have more than an inkling of what he meant.

Jaffa, of course, is justly famous for his argument that Shakespeare was a Platonic poet, the one envisaged by Socrates at the end of the *Symposium* who could write both comedies and tragedies. Shakespeare's political genius added Histories to his poetic repertoire. Jaffa made a simple but profound Platonic observation that in Shakespeare the difference between tragedy and comedy is determined by the presence or absence of philosophy. When a philosopher (or philosophic wisdom) is present, the play results in a comedy. Without a philosophic presence, it results in tragedy (philosophy, of course, is closer to comedy than tragedy). Shakespeare, according to Jaffa, accepted Machiavelli's critique of Christianity's detrimental influence on political life but disagreed with Machiavelli's radically new solution that required the lowering of the goals of political life to guarantee their actualization. Shakespeare, instead, looked to a revival of classical political philosophy as a solution.[1]

In January 2008 Jaffa wrote a new introduction to *Thomism and Aristotelianism* in preparation for a new edition that the Claremont Institute was planning to publish. Like many important issues after his "second sailing,"[2] Jaffa changed his mind about Thomas's intentions regarding Aristotle. When he published *Thomism and Aristotelianism* in 1952, Jaffa recounts, "I believed Thomas's intention was to make Aristotle safe for Christianity. I have since come to believe that his intention was to make Christianity safe for Aristotle." He notes that he will append to this reprinting of his first book an article, "Thomas Aquinas Meets Thomas Jefferson," which he published in 2006, that he seems to promise will explain in full this cryptic (and critical) turn-about in his thinking.[3] He adds another slightly less but still cryptic remark that he believed "the two Toms had more in common than either, in his time, would have wanted others to know. I have permitted them to shake hands under the table, practicing the art of writing that is a defense against persecution."[4]

Does Jaffa reveal what's behind the secret handshake? He certainly does not do so in any direct way in "Thomas

3

Aquinas Meets Thomas Jefferson." Jaffa did discuss Jefferson's 1813 letter to John Adams where Jefferson says that it would have been inconsistent in nature to have formed man for the social state and "not to have provided virtue and wisdom enough to manage the concerns of society." This means, not only that man is by nature a political being, but "that form of government is the best which provides the most effectually for a pure selection of these natural *aristoi* into the offices of government." Jaffa notes that Leo Strauss had said that this statement expressed "the very essence of the idea of the best regime in Plato and Aristotle, the very heart of classical political philosophy." With characteristic hyperbole, Jaffa remarks that "the theme of nature's fitting man for the social state, and providing virtue and talents for government, could hardly be more Aristotelian had it been written by Thomas Aquinas."

Finally, Jaffa has resort to George Washington, quoting the famous lines from his inaugural address: "[T]he foundations of our national policy," Washington said, "will be laid in the pure and immutable principles of private morality . . . . [T]here exists in the economy and course of nature an indissoluble union between virtue and happiness." Thus, Jaffa comments, according to the most authoritative statesman of the American founding era, "the actions of citizens and statesmen, whether private or public, must conform to 'the eternal rules of order and right.'" Jaffa rightly concludes with this rhetorical question: "Wherein does this differ from Thomas Aquinas's concept of the natural law, as the rational creature's participation in the eternal law?" And here Tom meets George. But no matter, Tom, and Tom, and George were working, albeit at different times, for the same eternal purpose, the moral foundations of civilized life.

Introduction

But what is odd is that we still haven't seen clearly what was concealed by the secret handshake, apart from the general reflection that the reasonable man's participation in the Eternal Law is at one and the same time the reasonable man's participation in the natural law. Divine law and natural law—as in the Declaration of Independence—become identical and its principles are accessible to reasoning men regardless of time, place, or religion. This is indeed a crucial insight!—but there is more.

In 2009, Professor Robert Kraynak published an article, "Moral Order in the Western Tradition: Harry Jaffa's Grand Synthesis of Athens, Jerusalem, and Peoria," to which Jaffa responded in a chapter in his last book, *Crisis of the Strauss Divided: Essays on Leo Strauss and Straussianism, East and West*. The title of the chapter, number seventeen, is a question: "Too Good to be True?" Here Jaffa takes up the argument where he left it off in "Aquinas Meets Jefferson." Aquinas's doctrine that the natural law represented the rational creature's participation in the eternal law, and the eternal law was, Jaffa continues,

> the law of God's government of the universe. By this doctrine Homo sapiens could by his reason (that is to say by the perfection of his reason) participate in God's government. In this, there is no necessary participation of positive divine law. According to Jefferson's statute [on Religious Liberty], a man's civil rights have no more dependence upon his religious opinions, than his opinion in physics or geometry. It seems shocking to suggest that Thomas Aquinas had similar views. Yet the possibility of the direct participation of human beings, possessed of reason (but not necessarily Christian faith) in the divine government of the universe, would certainly seem to

5

entitle them to an equal possibility to participate in civil government. This would mean, for example, that Jews or Infidels, no less than Christians, had that right. This perfectly correct Jeffersonian inference from Thomas's premises is one that Thomas did not make and would no doubt have denied. He would have denied it for the same reason that Lincoln in 1858 denied any intention to make voters or jurors of Negroes or of permitting them to marry whites . . . . Lincoln's proximate goal was arresting the spread of slavery into the territories. To have advocated voting rights for Negroes in Illinois in 1858 before the Civil War would only have divided those who were united in their opposition to the extension of slavery. Lincoln made it clear that in his mind stopping the spread of slavery was only the first step on the road to ultimate extinction. He did not in 1858 address the question of what might become prudent when the end of that road was in sight. Similarly, Thomas was engaged in a great effort to bring reason (as distinct from unreasoning prejudice) into Christian doctrine. The benefits that might eventually accrue to Jews or Infidels from that effort were not something that he could prudently bring to the attention of inquisitors hunting for heretics to burn. This comparison illuminates the fact that at different times and places religious prejudice and racial prejudice are among the most powerful obstacles to reason that prudence must circumvent. Prudence counsels caution and indirection in the face of such obstacles, but compromises do not of themselves imply a lack of principles.[5]

Jaffa draws his greatest comparison here, not between the two Toms, but between the first Tom and Lincoln, where the greatest prejudice is not religious, but racial. We must always keep in mind, however, that Lincoln said his political philosophy was always that of Jefferson's and, in any case, the irrationality of both forms of prejudice inevitably lead to political tyranny. Now we know why the two Toms were shaking hands under the table—it was a matter of prudence. The revelation of the full extent of their thought would have been political dynamite. Prudence is therefore the center of the theological-political question; it is at the heart of natural right, which, according to Aristotle, has everywhere the same force or power, but is everywhere changeable. The statesman, the man of practical wisdom, can mediate between what is eternally just and what is possible under changing circumstances. In order to know what is best under a variety of circumstances *phronimoi* must know what is best simply. Prudence is a moral virtue, both theoretical and practical.

Jaffa's last word on prudence caused quite a stir among so-called Eastern Straussians, a faction within the students of Strauss led by Professor Harvey Mansfield and the late Allan Bloom. This sect within Straussianism seems to believe that modernity succeeded both in destroying natural right and rendering prudence superfluous. In post-Machiavellian regimes, natural rights had become the "low but solid" substitute for natural right. Self-preservation would henceforth be the object of government—or in the case of Locke, property and the emancipation of acquisition. The distinction between ancients and moderns was for the East an eidetic bridge that could never be crossed, and those who believed it could were simply uninitiated in the mysteries of esotericism.

Jaffa reevaluated his analysis of Aristotelian natural right, concluding that for Aristotle, prudence and natural right were one and the same. Since natural right was a *part of political right* and was everywhere changeable even though it everywhere had the same force or power, prudence or practical wisdom, the political virtue par excellence, must be the same, if not identical, with natural right. "The prudence of the Declaration is the prudence of Aristotle and Lincoln," Jaffa wrote, "because there are not two kinds of prudence. While the manifestations of prudence are as many as the circumstances in which prudent action is possible, the virtue itself remains one and the same. This is why regarding Aristotle and Locke as representing opposing and contradictory philosophic doctrines is mistaken. The assumption that there is such a difference is the nerve of the difference between Eastern and Western Straussians."[6]

Even before Jaffa had uttered the heresy about prudence and natural right, he had committed an even greater heresy when he claimed that he had discovered Aristotle in the Declaration of Independence, a discovery that was made possible, as he clearly admits, by his "second sailing."[7] In a review of *A New Birth of Freedom*, Professor Charles Kesler, charged that Jaffa was "strangely silent" about the fact that he had given a "remarkably different" account of the American founding than he had in *Crisis of the House Divided* in 1959. Jaffa denied the charge; whether the denial was altogether fair to Kesler can be questioned. In any case, Jaffa remarks,

> I do not think that I have been as silent, or strangely so, as Professor Kesler seems to think. That the Founding, which Lincoln inherited, was dominated by an Aristotelian Locke—or a Lockean Aristotle—has been a conspicuous theme of my writing since 1987. It has gone largely unnoticed because it contradicts the conventional wisdom of certain academic establishments. Like the 'Purloined Letter,' however, it has been in plain sight all along.

8

After speaking of our unalienable rights, to secure which governments are instituted, the Declaration of Independence goes on to say that 'whenever any form of government becomes destructive of these ends, it is the right of the people to alter or abolish it, and to institute new government, laying its foundations on such principles and organizing its powers in such form, as to them seem most likely to effect their safety and happiness.' Notice that in the second institution, or reinstitution of government, 'rights' become 'ends.' And these ends are now said to be 'Safety' and 'Happiness,' the alpha and omega of political life in Aristotle's *Politics*. In one form or another, the metamorphosis of Lockean 'rights' into Aristotelian 'ends' (or vice versa) recurs in many of the documents of the founding.[8]

After his "second sailing," Harry Jaffa realized that Thomas Aquinas's intention was "to make Christianity safe for Aristotle," at the same time he realized that his most important task was to make Locke safe for America.

* * * * * * * * * * * *

A Note to the Reader

Much effort in the following volume has been dedicated to ensuring that Harry Jaffa's important discoveries after his "second sailing" have been taken into account when discussing the three books that form the main topic of this investigation, *Crisis of the House Divided, A New Birth of Freedom,* and *Crisis of the Strauss Divided*, all aiming at a commentary on the Gettysburg Address and the Second Inaugural. This applies especially to his discussion of the matter contained in the epigram that stands at head of the Introduction, Aristotle's view of natural right and prudence and how it influenced the American founding. Jaffa's view on this subject, like almost everything he wrote, is revolutionary. In the light of the discussion of natural right in Book V of the Ethics, I believe Aristotle would agree with Jaffa's interpretation that wherever political justice is possible, its prudent application is also possible. Thus, Jaffa's conclusion that for Aristotle, natural right and prudence are one and the same seems itself eminently prudent and is not restricted by any imaginary boundary that separates ancients and moderns.

In the three works under consideration, Jaffa made frequent references and analyses of the *Dred Scott* decision, a decision that played a decisive role in the politics of the 1850s and 1860s. In commentating on Jaffa's works it was necessary to follow and comment on his analyses of *Dred Scott*. Everyone but the casual reader will realize that I have not repeated any arguments, but I have extended and elaborated upon the discussions that Jaffa himself offered. Jaffa revised his understanding of that infamous case, and I was compelled to follow and comment on his important revisions and his deeper understanding.

Chapter One

HARRY JAFFA DEFENDS
A NEW BIRTH OF FREEDOM

Professor Michael P. Zuckert, not a friendly critic of Harry
Jaffa, reviewed *A New Birth of Freedom*, noting that, although
the author claims it is "the sequel to *Crisis of the House Divided*," its thesis "contradicts many of [its] central points."
"[O]ne is justified," Zuckert concludes, "that the *New Birth*
that appeared in 2000 is not the same book Jaffa promised
and projected in 1958. And yet, Jaffa presents *New Birth* as
the promised sequel."[1] There is not a strict requirement, of
course, that a sequel, agree with its prequel. In the interval
between the publication of *Crisis* and *A New Birth of Freedom*, Jaffa learned something important. We noted this in the
"Introduction" as his "second sailing," the central importance
of the "theological-political" question. He wrote about this in
an article in 1987.[2] Zuckert did, however, make some useful
observations, among them, as already noted in the Introduction, that the chapter on the Gettysburg Address doesn't deliver a commentary on the speech as promised but focuses on
the "self-evident truth" that "all men are created equal," and
sustains that focus throughout the entire book. Zuckert also

reveals Jaffa's connection to Leo Strauss and his interpretation of Plato's *Laws* from a close reading of the titles of chapters four and five, "The Mind of Lincoln's Inaugural and the Argument and Action of the Debate that Shaped It." Zuckert helpfully points out that Strauss's book-length commentary was entitled "*The Argument and Action of Plato's Laws.*"

In the "Preface" to *A New Birth* Jaffa responded "to the many who reproach me for the length of the interval between the alpha and the omega of this project, I can only reply that it corresponds closely to the distance in time that separated Plato's *Republic* from his *Laws*. One can claim a resemblance to the great without laying any claim to their greatness!" Thus, it is easy to conclude, as critics have, that Jaffa here indicates that the relationship between the *Republic* and the *Laws* is the same as that between *Crisis* and *A New Birth of Freedom*, the philosophic or best regime to the second best or political regime. Careful examination, however, disappoints these early expectations.

Jaffa mentions that *Crisis of the House Divided* was written in the form of a "disputed question." That form is not suitable for a "commentary on the Gettysburg address," Jaffa alleges, which is a "speech within a drama." As such, "[i]t can no more be interpreted apart from that drama than, let us say, a speech of Hamlet or Macbeth can be interpreted apart from *Hamlet* or *Macbeth*." Anyone who is familiar with Strauss's account of the *Laws* understands how the action of the dialogue (the "drama") is essential to understanding its "argument" (the *logos*). But in what sense is the *logos* within a drama? The *logoi* of course are the speeches of Abraham Lincoln without which the actions or tragedy of the Civil War cannot be understood. "Lincoln is the tragic hero. The Civil War is itself an outcome of tragic flaws—birthmarks, so to speak—of the infant nation." Jaffa meets a potential objection: "It may be objected that history is not poetry and that I have confused them. To this I would reply, as I think Lincoln would reply—or rather, as Lincoln in effect did reply—that the place of necessity in great poetry imposed by the art of the poet may be occupied by a providential order in history revealed in the speeches of the tragic hero. Lincoln became the prophetic statesman of a people, like Israel of old, whose failings and sufferings were intrinsic to the uniqueness of their role as a chosen people."³

According to Zuckert the deepest connection to Plato's *Laws* is that "*New Birth* represents the sort of theologization of politics that Plato presents in *Laws*."⁴ While Jaffa accords with Strauss's opposition to the "four horsemen of the modern apocalypse," "historicism, positivism, relativism [and] nihilism," in a variety of ways, Zuckert claims, he "clearly breaks with features of Strauss's thinking," especially as he was a "thinker of dualities—ancients and moderns, Jerusalem and Athens, philosophy and poetry, the city and man." At one fell swoop Jaffa, by "theologizing" politics, has collapsed at least "Athens and Jerusalem, poetry and philosophy, and perhaps has even tried to cross that imaginary eidetic bridge that separates "ancients and moderns." "What Strauss has put asunder," Zuckert laments, "Jaffa attempts to join together."⁵

Did Harry Jaffa Differ from Strauss by "Theologizing Politics" in A New Birth Of Freedom?

Zuckert is perhaps not sufficiently answered by pointing out that Strauss used as the epigraph to his book *The Argument and Action of Plato's* Laws a quotation from Avicenna: ". . . the treatment of prophecy and the Divine law is contained in . . . the *Laws*." Was Strauss serious that "prophecy" was treated in the *Laws*? And "Divine law?" This would seem to imply more than "theologizing." Or does it? Perhaps Strauss was merely acknowledging that Avicenna had publicly conceded that the *Laws* was about prophecy and Divine law because in Islam, the law was settled and could not be questioned or interpreted apart from orthodoxy whereas prophecy was open to philosophy. I suspect this is Strauss's exoteric message but is it the real message of his commentary and, if so, does the real message thereby violate one of his alleged "dualities." In *Crisis of the Strauss Divided*, Jaffa refers to Strauss's opening statement about the Declaration of Independence in *Natural Right and History* (about which we will have much more to say later). Jaffa states:

> When Strauss asked, 'Does this nation in its maturity still cherish the faith in which it was conceived and raised?' he was asking the question which was the core of all Lincoln's speeches from 1854 until his death. . . . Lincoln had spoken of the principles of the declaration as 'our ancient faith,' and had appealed to those principles in the manner of an Old Testament prophet, calling upon his people to return to the right way. Like Lincoln (above all in his second inaugural), Strauss too would express the meaning of natural right in the language of

the Bible, for the theme of *Natural Right and History* is expressed *a priori* in its epigraphs, which are taken from II Samuel and I Kings. I do not pretend for a moment to speak for Leo Strauss, but I am perfectly convinced that Strauss shared the conviction that Lincoln's appeal, in his greatest speeches, to the Declaration of Independence and to the Bible—to Reason and to Revelation—was the very model of wise statesmanship at the highest level. It was, in particular, a model of that statesmanship in its bearing upon the crisis of the West, the crisis of that civilization constituted at its core by the coming together of doctrines derived from the Bible and from the idea of autonomous human reason. The connection between prophecy and statesmanship, which Strauss himself first learned from the Islamic scholars of Plato, and which he first taught to me in 1945, was the ground upon which my study of Lincoln began.[6]

The Bible does not know nature, but its epigrams express an awareness of natural right.[7] It has been said that the Old Testament text assiduously and explicitly avoids all reference to nature. If this is true, it would be a philosophic book because it would be fully conscious of the need to avoid the concept of nature. Strauss did indeed learn about "prophecy and statesmanship" from Islamic scholars. At another point, Jaffa makes an even more revealing statement when he notes that "Lincoln's recovery of the Founding corresponded closely with the Maimonidean recovery of the rational origins of prophecy."[8]

Jaffa frequently pointed to Romans 2:14 to show a philosophic basis for the New Testament: "When Gentiles ('έθνη = pagans) who have not the law [of Moses] do by nature (φύσει) what the law [of Moses] requires, they are a law unto themselves." The Old Testament was the law for a particular people given by a universal God. Still, Israel was an ancient city. Christianity was a universal religion appealing to all nations. Jaffa pointed out that the book of Matthew begins with a genealogy of Jesus stretching back "blood of blood and flesh of flesh" for 3 X 14 generations. As the account of Matthew continues, however, and "Jesus is speaking to his disciples, and a messenger comes to him, and tells him that his mother and his brothers are waiting to see him. 'Who are my mother and my brothers?' Jesus asks. Then, pointing to the disciples, says 'There are my mother and my brothers.'" The point of this passage, Jaffa concludes here and other places, is that descent by blood is replaced by faith in the New Testament, a position that was taken by Lincoln in a speech given in July, 1858, which should be considered an extended commentary on an infamous line in a speech given by Stephen Douglas in June, 1857, entitled "Kansas, Utah, and the *Dred Scott* Decision," in which he alleged, not for the first or last time, that America was founded on the "white man's basis." But the resounding thesis of his speech was that "No one can vindicate the character, motives and conduct of the signers of the Declaration of Independence, except upon the hypothesis that they referred to the white race alone, and not to the African, when they declared all men to have been created equal—that *they were speaking of British subjects on this continent being equal to British subjects born and residing in Great Britain*—that they were entitled to the same inalienable rights, and among them were enumerated life, liberty and the pursuit of happiness. The declaration was adopted for the purpose of justifying the colonists, in the eyes of the civilized world, in withdrawing their allegiance from the British crown, and dissolving the connection with the mother country. In this point of view the Declaration of Independence is in perfect harmony with all the events of the Revolution."[9]

Lincoln's extended answer to Douglas came in a speech addressing an audience made up primarily of recent immigrants, on July 10, 1858, when he remarked that:

> We have besides these men—descended by blood from our ancestors—among us perhaps half our people who are from Europe—German, Irish, French and Scandinavians—men that have come from Europe themselves, or whose ancestors have come hither and settled here, finding themselves our equals in all things. If they look back through history to trace their connection with those days by blood, they find they have none, they cannot carry themselves back into that glorious epoch and make themselves feel that they are part of us, but when they look through that old Declaration of Independence they find that those old men say that "We hold these truths to be self-evident, that all men are created equal," and then they feel that moral sentiment in that day evidences their relation to those men, that it is the father of all moral principle in them, and that they have a right to claim it as though they were blood of the blood and flesh of the flesh of the men who wrote that Declaration, and so they are. That is the electric cord in the Declaration that links the hearts of patriotic and liberty-loving men together, that will link those patriotic hearts as long as the love of freedom exists in the minds of men throughout the world.[10]

Jaffa comments that "[t]his is the teaching of the Declaration of Independence no less than of the Gospels."[11] The principles of the American founding had made it possible to reconcile the demand of reason and revelation on a moral and political level—that is, on the only level in which it is possible to solve the question of reason and revelation. On the highest level, the question of what perfects or completes human life, reason (the life of philosophy) or revelation (the life of faith), seems impossible to resolve. Reason is incapable of refuting the possibility of revelation and revelation evidently cannot deny the possibility of reason. But on a moral and political level reason and revelation can agree. And the conditions for this agreement were almost providential. The ground for that agreement was prepared by Locke and it took the form of the "Laws of Nature and Nature's God," and "a decisive influence . . . was Locke's *Letter Concerning Toleration*," which Jaffa also notes "inspired Madison's *Memorial and Remonstrance*" and "was a principal resource for Jefferson in drafting the Virginia Statute for Religious Freedom." These two documents, Jaffa comments, "I believe are the greatest documents of human freedom in all human history."

The Virginia Statute states "that our civil rights have no dependence on our religious opinions any more than opinions in physics or geometry."

> No government in the history of the world had ever admitted or acknowledged such a proposition. The ancient city understood itself as a creation of its gods (or God). The Israelite polity celebrated in the Old Testament, whatever may be distinctive in its monotheism, is typical of other ancient cities in its proclaimed dependence upon a divine lawgiver. However universal the Hebrew Deity was believed to be, the Mosaic legislation was particular. In the ancient city, citizenship, or membership in a

polity, is identical in principle with obedience to the god or gods of that polity. No distinction was possible between civil and religious liberty. When the Constitution of the United States in 1787 declared that there should never be a religious test for office it effected the greatest change ever in the relationship of man to government.[12]

Twelve years before the publication of these lines, Jaffa had made this surprising statement in *A New Birth of Freedom*: "The most fundamental of the assumptions underlying the American political tradition is not set forth in the Declaration of Independence. Rather, it is to be found in the magisterial exordium of the Virginia Statute of Religious Liberty, in the assertion that 'Almighty God hath created the mind free.' When the Declaration says, 'We hold these truths to be self-evident', it assumes that the minds holding the truths do so on the basis of that metaphysical freedom asserted in the Virginia Statute. We must understand precisely in what that metaphysical freedom of the mind consists, because the moral and political freedom asserted on behalf of mankind is grounded in it."[13]

Harry Jaffa Asks a Plato Question and Asks Aristotle's Help

A question closely related to the statement just quoted was also posed by Jaffa:

We must face the reality. . . that in the long experience of mankind, the self-evident truths of the Declaration of Independence had never, before 1776, been the basis of the experiment of popular self-government. This in itself is sufficient to raise the question of whether it was utopian to think that mere abstract truth could serve as the basis of an actual political regime. It is to ask the question that Plato himself asked, but did not answer, of whether natural right could become political right.[14]

If we read carefully, I say neither Lincoln nor Jaffa seem to answer Plato's question. Lincoln in his Dred Scott speech of 1857 says the Declaration provides a "standard maxim for free society, which should be familiar to all, and revered by all; constantly looked to, constantly labored for, and even though never perfectly attained, constantly approximated, and thereby constantly spreading and deepening its influence, and augmenting the happiness and value of life to all people of all colors everywhere."[15] This is a perfectly Platonic speech—it is the celebration of a platonic "idea." There can be participation but not perfection. This, of course, is the moderation or limitation of Platonic politics. The principles of the Declaration, according to Lincoln, will never be perfected, but they can be approximated. Platonic natural right can never be translated into political right in the same sense as Aristotelian natural right. But from the point of view of today's crucial task of opposing the corrosive forces of modernity, the differences between Plato and Aristotle pale into insignificance compared to their agreements about the moral foundations of political life that are derived from the principles of human nature, those principles that both Lincoln and Jaffa were certain were embodied in the Declaration of Independence.

Both Plato and Aristotle teach eternal principles, those principles necessary to combat the relativism, historicism, positivism and nihilism that infect our age. Jaffa's understanding of the theological-political question which he came to understand more deeply in the years between the publication of *Crisis of the House Divided* and *A New Birth of Freedom* led him to the conclusion that the "Laws of Nature and of Nature's God" in the Declaration rest on the twin pillars of reason and revelation and the defense of the principles of the American founding is today the most powerful defense of America, and America is almost certainly the last best hope of the West.

A New Birth Of Freedom *is a Dialectic between Plato and Aristotle on the Question of Natural Right and Political Right*

Jaffa's *A New Birth of Freedom* is profitably read as a dialectic between Plato and Aristotle on the question of how (or whether) natural right can become political right. Jaffa, I firmly believe, was always a Platonist; but he saw Aristotle as a valuable and prudent ally in the war against nihilism. Eventually, he saw that Aristotle's prudence was, in fact, identical with natural right and, in that momentous discovery, natural right became political right in a way that provided a decisive answer to Plato's question.

But there is an intriguing passage that appears, quite surprisingly, some two hundred pages after Jaffa asks the question which Plato doesn't answer. And this passage emphatically claims that Lincoln *did translate natural right into political right* and points directly to the Peoria speech, a speech that took place four years before the Dred Scott speech. Lincoln in the Peoria speech reports that "according to our ancient faith, the just powers of government are derived from the consent of the governed.[16] Now the relation of masters and slaves is, PRO TANTO, a total violation of this principle. The master not only governs the slave without his consent; but he governs him by a set of rules altogether different from those which he prescribes for himself. Allow ALL the governed an equal voice in the government, and that, and that only is self-government."[17] Jaffa remarks that this last sentence is Lincoln's "single most revealing utterance of his life on the Declaration as a proposition of political right." "Although revealing," Jaffa continues, "it is also Delphic when placed in the context of his other antebellum utterances, which seem to contradict such an unqualified commitment. Let us be clear, however, that Lincoln thought that the just powers government are derived from the consent of ALL the governed, with no exceptions. Let us also be clear that Lincoln did not mean consent in any passive sense. He meant, as he said, that it entailed an equal voice in the government. He meant democracy in the fullest sense."[18]

This "Delphic" revelation is discussed in chapter five of *A New Birth of Freedom*, "The Mind of Lincon's Inaugural— II," and is preceded by a discussion of social compact "as we discussed in chapter 1." What the discussion in chapter one emphasized was the natural law limitations on majority rule. This, according to Jaffa, was recognized by Lincoln in his First Inaugural when he confirmed what the principles of the Declaration make "abundantly clear," that "the authority of the majority ceases when it denies to a minority any of the fundamental rights implicit in the original unanimous consent upon which the majority authority is based."[19] In response to Douglas's popular sovereignty position, Lincoln's reasoning was clear according to Jaffa:

> A vote for slavery is a vote to abrogate the initial understanding that brought society into existence. It is no

more consistent with the principles of self-government than a vote to establish one religion and forbid the free exercise of any other. One cannot decide between Protestantism and Catholicism, or Christianity and Judaism, by vote. In such an event, the decision of the majority has no rational claim to obedience. It could be enforced, if at all, only tyrannically, and it would be an invitation to rebellion and anarchy.[20]

Lincoln's principles were fully settled by the time of the Peoria speech in 1854. It appears that the only changes he made between 1854, and the First Inaugural were in the rhetorical strategies he chose to employ, and those were dictated by the ebb and flow of changing political circumstances. His principles were, like those of the Declaration itself, unchanging.

Lincoln Demonstrates His Statesmanship at a Critical Juncture

November 8, 1861, brought the United States and Britain to the brink of war. The Trent Affair was deemed by Britain as an act of war and an expedition was sent to the Canadian border to prepare for an invasion of the United States. Lincoln's cabinet, especially Secretary of State William Seward, was eager for war. His fantastic reasoning was that war with Britain would unite America and the South would forget succession in its enthusiasm to wage war against Britain. Never mind that the Slaveocracy had endeavored to bring Britain into the Civil War on its side and, in fact, the Trent Affair was part of the effort to enlist the help of Britain. Field-Marshall Viscount Wolseley recounts in his *The Story of a Soldier's Life* how Britain began to prepare for hostile action. More importantly for our purposes, however, he describes with great accuracy Lincoln's statesmanship in the Trent matter:

> One of the very shrewdest of men and most sagacious of statesmen, Mr. Abraham Lincoln, was then President, and was determined to crush what the people of the Northern States regarded as the rebellion of the Sothern States. But he was wise enough to realize that he could not do so if our fleet, by keeping open the Southern ports, enabled the young Confederacy to obtain from Europe everything they required for their war. Without doubt, thousands of recruits from all parts of Europe would have poured in through the ports we should keep open. He therefore most wisely determined to disown the over-zealous act of a by no means far-seeing naval captain, and accordingly, with all due apologies for the insult offered to our flag, he delivered over to us the envoys who had been taken by force from a British merchant ship. Thus ended an episode that must have brought on a terrible war if the United States had been ruled then by an ordinary man.[21]

A two-front war against the Slaveocracy and the powerful British Army and Naval forces would have been a disaster for America. Wolseley, an experienced soldier who would have led the British invasion from Canada clearly had sympathies congruent with those of the Slaveocracy, and spent time interviewing Generals Lee, Jackson, and Longstreet. America's navy was no match for the British fleet. As Wolseley truly noted, Lincoln's decision was "most wise." Indeed, it was a genuine act of statesmanship!

Chapter One

Jaffa Returns to the Beginning

Harry Jaffa contends that: Nothing is more important for understanding Strauss than the place of the Declaration of Independence in the beginning of *Natural Right and History*, where Strauss quotes: "We hold these truths to be self-evident, that all men are created equal, that they are endowed by the Creator with certain unalienable Rights, that among these are Life, Liberty, the pursuit of Happiness," and then comments: "The nation dedicated to this proposition has now become, no doubt partly as a consequence of this dedication, the most powerful and prosperous of the nations of the earth. Does this nation in its maturity still cherish the faith in which it was conceived and raised? Does it still hold those 'truths to be self-evident?'"

Jaffa notes that Strauss never returned to these questions nor did he answer them directly. Rather, *Natural Right and History* was a sustained account of how history replaced nature in Western civilization. "It is of some interest," Jaffa recalls, "that the original Walgreen Lecture (at which I was present) delivered in the fall of 1949, had a different beginning from the first chapter of *Natural Right and History*, published in 1953. In 1949 Strauss began by quoting a medieval aphorism, *Solet Aristoteles quaerere pugnam*, Aristotle is accustomed to seeking a fight. Strauss then promptly reenacted the role of Aristotle, in plunging into his war against historicism, and its misbegotten offspring, relativism, positivism and nihilism. But in 1949 he made no reference to the Declaration."[22]

Jaffa was willing to take credit for the appearance of the Declaration in 1953, while at the same time denying any responsibility. "Between 1949 and 1953," Jaffa recounts, "Strauss apparently decided that the fate of the Declaration of Independence was an authentic representation of the fate of Natural Right. Whether 'Expediency and Morality in the Lincoln Douglas Debates' (1951)[23] had anything to do with this decision, I cannot say. It is notable, however, that although Strauss in 1953 gives the words [of the Declaration] in direct quotation, he uses Lincoln's words at Gettysburg as his own, without quotation marks. In speaking of the nation's dedication to a proposition, and of the faith in which it was conceived and raised, he speaks with Lincoln's voice as if it were his own."[24] The observation that Strauss was speaking in Lincoln's voice is an accurate insight into Strauss's thought concerning Lincoln and the fate of natural right. It is my belief that Jaffa's essay published in 1951 did in fact influence Strauss's decision to include a reference to the Declaration at the beginning of *Natural Right and History*, and if Jaffa is right about Strauss adopting Lincoln's voice—as he almost certainly is—he was also encouraging Jaffa to take up the defense of natural right on Lincolnian principles.

Zuckert points out that Thomas West, "a close student of Jaffa," notes that the first two chapters of *New Birth of Freedom* are devoted to (1) natural right and (2) history, the principal topics of the first two chapters of Leo Strauss's *Natural Right and History*. Zuckert acknowledged West's judgment that *New Birth* was made possible by the work of Leo Strauss. Zuckert is quick to note, however, that "[t]here are . . . a number of strong counter-currents to those obtrusively Straussian elements of *New Birth*."[25] The main counter-current that concerns us here is the one Zuckert identifies in the "Introduction" to *Natural Right and History*, when Strauss quotes from the Declaration of Independence. Zuckert correctly points out that Strauss does not say that that the principles of the Declaration are true, but he does ask "Does this nation in its maturity still cherish the faith in which it was conceived and raised?" Recognizing the Lincolnian strophes here, Zuckert also thinks this is a condemnation of Lincoln, and to prove it Zuckert quotes from *Natural Right and History*: "Since men are then unequal in regard to human perfection, i.e., in the decisive respect, equal rights for all appeared to the classics as most unjust. They contend that some men are by nature superior to others and therefore, according to natural right, the rulers of others."[26] Zuckert concludes from this passage that "Strauss is closer to those who deny the truth of the proposition in the Declaration than he is to those like [Carl] Becker who consider them meaningless, or those like Jefferson and Lincoln, who hold them to be true."[27]

Zuckert's indictment here of Jefferson and Lincoln is surprising; it is not only mistaken, but unjust! Before we return to Jaffa's answer to Zuckert, we are compelled to expose one of Zuckert's deliberate misrepresentations of Lincoln which bears directly on the question of justice. In his recent book, *A Nation So Conceived: Abraham Lincoln and the Paradox of Democratic Sovereignty*, commenting on Lincoln's Peoria address, Zuckert makes the case that rights, rather than equality, were always Lincoln's main concern. Denying that equality was the central core of the American founding has been a long-standing project for Zuckert. In the pursuit of this project, Zuckert, I say, intentionally misrepresents Lincoln's position. "We can understand," Zuckert proclaims, Lincoln's "reasons for opposing Douglas's effort at a statesmanlike settlement as well as his reasons for not going further in an abolitionist direction only by attending to what he says about the monstrous injustice of slavery itself."[28] Zuckert, then, as is his wont, constructs a syllogism that concludes "therefore [slavery] is unjust because it is a denial of equal rights, a denial of the rights of self-ownership."[29] "Equality of rights," Zuckert continues, "is, said Lincoln, 'the sheet anchor of American republicanism' and 'the relation of masters and slaves . . . a total violation of this principle.'"[30] Lincoln certainly believed that the master-slave relation was a violation of "equality of rights," but he did not say that "equality of rights" was "the sheet anchor of American republicanism." Even a casual reading of the Peoria speech shows that Lincoln said that "consent" is the "leading principle—the sheet anchor of American republicanism." After saying this, Lincoln immediately quoted the Declaration of Independence, beginning with the "self-evident" truth that "all men are created equal" and ending with—and emphasizing—that the "JUST POWERS" of government are derived "FROM THE CONSENT OF THE GOVERNED."[31] Equality and consent, of course, are the reciprocal requirements of the social compact theory of the Declaration as understood both by Lincoln and the founders. As we will see in due course, Zuckert also denies that social compact was ever a legitimate part of the American founding, although it was widely accepted by the founding generation, and in particular by James Madison who asserted that "all power in just & free Gover[nmen]t is derived from compact."[32]

As early as 1987, Zuckert had begun his campaign to deny the central importance of equality to the American founding, when he boldly argued that when the Declaration of Independence proclaims, "We hold these truths to be self-evident," it means the "truths" are "true" only because "we" hold them. We do not hold them because they are objectively or intrinsically true or grounded in natural right; they are "our truths" and by that fact merely conventional, and certainly not derived from the "laws of nature and nature's God."[33] Professor Zuckert has in the intervening years—quite understandably—attempted to dissemble his views without changing his opinions on the question of equality in the Declaration. In a book published in 1996, he stated that "natural equality derives from . . . natural rights. Each person has rights to life, liberty, and the pursuit of happiness." The possession of these natural rights means, of course, that no "other person could naturally be the ruler of any individual" who possesses these rights because such authority would be inconsistent with the possession and exercise of those rights and would imply that the individuals do not actually possess those rights. "Thus," Zuckert confidently concludes, "the primordial possession of such wide-ranging natural rights implies natural equality."[34] Zuckert tries to save this from becoming a circular argument by referring to the "primordial possession" of "wide-ranging natural rights" which "*implies* natural equality" (emphasis added). The possession of natural rights of an unspecified source (the Bill of Rights understood as "organic law"?) thus implies the existence of "natural rights." The circle doesn't seem to have been broken. We presume Zuckert's "primordial possession" is an attempt to supply the equivalent of a "self-evident truth." Without this "equivalent" the argument necessarily ends in aporia. The foundation of "rights" cannot be "rights;" it must be the "self-evident truth" of equality.

Jaffa has explained the meaning of equality as a "self-evident truth" many times in his voluminous works. In fact, no topic is so prevalent in his corpus as the meaning of "the self-evident truth" that "all men are created equal." In my own rehearsal of the argument, I have added some facets that are directed especially at Zuckert's fraudulent use of Strauss's account of inequality that he cited from *Natural Right and History*. As we noted above, Jaffa proved beyond cavil that

Strauss's citation of the Declaration at the beginning of that book, and Strauss's use of Lincoln's voice as his own, which Jaffa cogently pointed out, meant that Strauss accepted Lincoln's view of natural right as the authentic view, contrary to what Zuckert would have us believe. And, as we will see in short order, Zuckert fails to understand that Strauss himself admits that *Natural Right and History* was not his last word on ancients and moderns and consequently not his last word on natural right.[35]

A self-evident truth, as Jaffa has explained many times in his writings, contains the proof of its truth within the terms of the statement itself and is incapable of any further proof. For example, the axiom that "things equal to the same thing are equal to each other," is a self-evident truth. Anyone who understands the terms "same" and "other" cannot fail at the same time to understand the meaning of "equal" or fail to affirm the truth of the axiom. It is an objective statement of the relation of things in the world. Any person of ordinary common sense would recognize the truth of the statement immediately upon hearing it even though he would be unable to formulate the axiom in the first instance. This statement was true before the axiom was discovered and will continue to be true even if the axiom is forgotten or its truth denied. In other words, its existence or truth is independent of human thought or creation.[36]

Self-evident truths concerning justice and injustice would seem to be something entirely different from geometrical proofs. Lincoln, however, continued to insist that "the principles of Jefferson are the definitions and axioms of free society."[37] Some intelligent writers have noted that Lincoln might have made an important distinction between axioms and definitions which are "self-evident" truths and "propositions" which, in Euclidean geometry, which we know Lincoln studied,[38] are not self-evident truths but require further proof. Lincoln used the term "proposition" as early as the Lyceum speech in 1838 to describe the Declaration, but more importantly for our purposes, he did so in the Gettysburg address, in the memorable phrase that "our fathers brought forth, upon this continent, a new nation, conceived in liberty, and dedicated to the proposition that 'all men are created equal.'" Five years earlier in the Dred Scott speech Lincoln, as we have seen, had called the Declaration "a standard maxim." These are issues that will be addressed in the chapter devoted to the Gettysburg Address. Jaffa doesn't address this issue directly, but I believe he does answer it.[39]

Lincoln, of course, regarded Jefferson as "the most distinguished politician of our history," who "was, is, and perhaps will continue to be." His principal role as "a chief actor in the revolution" was as "the author of the Declaration of Independence."[40] In reference to Zuckert's use of Strauss's statement that "since men are . . . unequal in regard to human perfection. . . [and] by nature superior to others. . . according to natural right [are] the rulers of other," Jefferson certainly recognized that there are inequalities among human beings, not the least of which are inequalities of strength, beauty, intelligence, and social and moral capacity. *It is therefore equally a self-evident truth that all men are not created equal in all respects.* The Declaration, of course, addresses the question of political rule, and it is in this regard that the self-evident truth of human equality is applicable.[41] Whatever inequalities exist among human beings—however measured—none are great enough to make one human being, or class, or caste naturally the rulers of others. As Jefferson noted, "the mass of mankind has not been born with saddles on their backs, nor a favored few booted and spurred, ready to ride them legitimately, by the grace of God."[42] If some were born with saddles and others born with boots and spurs, that would indicate Nature's or God's intention that those with boots and spurs should ride on the backs of those born with saddles. That was the argument that was made for the divine right of kings—"the grace of God." But the self-evident truth about the human species is that no human being occupies a position with respect to other human beings that any human being occupies with respect to every horse. The inequality between human beings and horses makes every human being by nature the ruler of every horse. The same inequalities do not exist within the human species. As Jefferson noted, "because Sir Isaac Newton was superior to others in understanding, he was not therefore lord of the person or property of others."[43] Social compact as it emerged in human consciousness, not only made republican government possible, it also foretold the end of divine right monarchy and slavery. In the Peoria address Lincoln made the point that the case that the "Divine right of Kings" and the argument for slavery "are precisely alike; and it is but natural that they should find similar arguments to sustain them."[44] In the seventh debate with Douglas on Oct. 15, 1858, Lincoln assailed Douglas's "don't care" stance on slavery: That is the "real issue," Lincoln contended

> that will continue in this country when these poor tongues of Judge Douglas and myself shall be silent. It is the eternal struggle between these two principles— right and wrong—throughout the world. They are the two principles that have stood face to face from the beginning of time; and will ever continue to struggle. The one is the common right of humanity and the other the

divine right of kings. It is the same principle in whatever shape it develops itself. It is the same spirit that says, 'You work and toil and earn bread, and I'll eat it.' No matter in what shape it comes, whether from the mouth of a king who seeks to bestride the people of his own nation and live by the fruit of their labor, or from one race of men as an apology for enslaving another race, it is the same tyrannical principle.[45]

Jaffa wrote about divine right monarchy and tyranny in chapter two of *A New Birth of Freedom*: "The divine right of kings, in the comprehensive sense of the right to rule others without their consent," Jaffa states, "predominated within Western civilization until the American Revolution." He then makes some surprising observations. "To have done so for nearly eighteen hundred years after the birth of Christianity," he muses, "would make it appear that civilized mankind, with the possible exception of a few philosophers, had during all that time lived in ignorance of the rights announced in the Declaration of Independence." What other conclusion could come readily to mind other than "the divine right of kings must therefore have had a plausibility not easily visible today." This bears on the revolutionary character of the American founding: "We must understand that plausibility in order to take the measure of the magnitude of the change in human consciousness achieved in the American founding—and thus the magnitude of the stakes at risk in the American Civil War."[46]

It is not unimportant to note (again) that this statement appears in chapter two, the chapter that promised—but did not deliver—a commentary on the Gettysburg Address. What is more, Jaffa claims that Lincoln derived his understanding of the divine right of kings and tyranny mostly from the philosophic poetry of Shakespeare's English History plays, and the bulk of his discussion is about *Henry V*, but also *Macbeth*.[47]

Lincoln made these revealing statements in his Peoria address in 1854 when he believed he had been called to active service in the defense of America's founding principles. Almost alone, Lincoln saw that the repeal of the Kansas-Nebraska Act, orchestrated by his soon-to-be arch-rival Stephen A. Douglas, was tantamount to a repeal of the Declaration of Independence itself. Douglas declared that it was a matter for the territories and the states to determine by majority vote whether or not to approve slavery. Majority rule, he solemnly declaimed, was the sacred principle of democracy. If the majority finds it in its interest, then it will "vote it up;" if it does not, it will vote it down. Lincoln stated that his purpose was to determine "whether the repeal of the Missouri Compromise was right or wrong," concluding "it is wrong in its direct effect, letting slavery into Kansas and Nebraska" and "because of the monstrous injustice of slavery itself." It forces many good men "into an open war with the very fundamental principles of civil liberty—criticising the Declaration of Independence and insisting that there is no right principle of action but *self-interest*."[48] Majority rule, Lincoln insisted here and throughout his later debates with Douglas, was a part, but not the complete principle of republican government; rather republicanism required majority rule combined with minority rights. Lincoln firmly believed that the Declaration of Independence, in its reference to "the laws of nature and nature's God," had grounded its doctrines in a moral universe that put limitations on what could be done by the majority. In declaring that "all men are created equal" and "endowed by their Creator with certain unalienable rights," a Creator and a created universe are acknowledged. The universe is thus ordered, not random, and is therefore accessible to human reason. The order of the universe is presumably revealed to human reason in the form of self-evident truths and the deductions and conclusion impelled by those truths.[49] The self-evident truth that "all men are created equal" means that natural rights belong to individuals; consequently, there are no rights that do not carry concomitant obligations. This is a necessary result of the implicit fact that the Declaration rests on social compact.

Since republican government can only derive its "just powers" from the "consent of the governed," it must always operate within the confines of public opinion, and public opinion can sometimes be stubborn, intransigent, and is too often stubbornly irrational. This always poses a challenge to republican statesmanship, and it was a perilous public opinion that Lincoln confronted in the turbulent politics before the Civil War.

Some three years later, in March of 1860, Lincoln made a speech in New Haven, Connecticut that was remarkable for its candor. He contended that in the nation's history the only thing that had ever endangered "the perpetuity of this Union" was slavery. And, he added, "[w]henever this question shall be settled, it must be settled on some philosophical basis. No policy that does not rest upon some philosophical public opinion can be permanently maintained."[50] The "philosophical basis" that Lincoln was referring to was, of course, the Declaration of Independence. This is the only basis for a public opinion that can be "permanently maintained," because it is based on permanent principles embodied in the "laws of nature and nature's God." The opinions that support these permanent truths will not be permanently maintained without the constant attention of "opinion makers," republican statesman whose task it is to keep public opinion anchored to the founding principles.

But there are others, Lincoln said, who compete for the attention of the public mind. Not only Calhoun, the original protagonist, but his epigone Douglas, with his doctrine of "popular sovereignty" vie for attention, both seeking to undermine original principles. Lincoln says Douglas's doctrine "stands in the way of a permanent settlement" of the slavery question. For Douglas to succeed, Lincoln avers, "[t]here must be a change in public opinion, the public mind must be so far debauched as to square with this policy of caring not at all" whether slavery be voted up or down. "The people must come to consider this as 'merely a question of dollars and cents,' and to believe that in some places the Almighty has made Slavery necessarily eternal." "You are ready to say it cannot, but be not too fast," Lincoln responded to surprised audience reaction. "Remember what a long stride has been taken since the repeal of the Missouri Compromise!" "I venture to defy the whole [Democratic] party," Lincoln challenged, "to produce one man that ever uttered the belief that the Declaration did not apply to negroes, before the repeal of the Missouri Compromise! Four or five years ago we all thought negroes were men, and that when '*all men*' were named, negroes were included. But *the whole Democratic party has deliberately taken negroes from the class of men and put them in the class of brutes.* Turn it as you will, it is simply the truth! Don't be too hasty then in saying that the people cannot be brought to this new doctrine, but note that long stride."[51] This long stride, of course, was made possible by Douglas's "doctrine of popular sovereignty" which was a direct attack on the "philosophic basis" of public opinion that Lincoln saw in the repeal of the Kansas–Nebraska Act. Douglas's attempt to divorce the question of morality from the slavery question and to substitute a blatant appeal to interest in its place, is at one and the same time an attempt to divorce the Constitution from the Declaration.

Strauss Cites Thomas Jefferson on Natural Aristoi

Much has been made of a reference to Jefferson by Strauss in his essay "On Classical Political Philosophy," first published in 1945 and republished in *What is Political Philosophy?* in 1959. Strauss wrote "[as] Thomas Jeffersson put it," "That form of government is the best, which provides the most effectually for a pure selection of [the] natural *aristoi* into the offices of the government." (Strauss cites, in footnote nine, Letter of John Adams, October 28, 1813.)[52] It seems odd that Jaffa found it necessary to remind a scholar of Zuckert's rank of Strauss's quotation of Jefferson for his argument praising the "natural aristoi" as being those most suitable to occupy offices of trust in government and society. Jaffa points out an interesting fact and given Strauss's meticulous practice of the art of writing, it might prove to be significant: In the original, Jefferson poses the statement as a question, whereas Strauss presents it as a declarative statement. In doing so, does this mean that Strauss has adopted the statement as his own? Quite likely! After all, didn't a similar exegesis by Jaffa reveal that Strauss had adopted Lincoln's voice as his own in the opening paragraph of *Natural Right and History*?

"It would have been inconsistent in creation," Jefferson asserted in his letter to John Adams, "to have formed man for the social state and not to have provided virtue and wisdom enough to manage the concerns of society."[53] Thus Jefferson, in some sense, believed in the Aristotelian proposition that man is by nature a social or political animal. Jaffa wrote that this is "unsurpassed Aristotelianism. I do not see how one can fail to see the irrelevance of merely chronological divide between ancients and moderns." In other words, the ancients and modern distinction is merely a kind of historicism.[54] Jefferson also warns of a pseudo-aristocracy that claims wisdom and virtue as a title to rule, but in fact thinks wealth or power is an adequate substitute. It is a clear lesson of Aristotle's *Politics* that most regimes claiming to be aristocracies— the rule of the best—are in fact oligarchies, the rule of the rich. Only a regime, based on equality, providing equality of opportunity with no class or caste barriers to advancement based solely on natural talent and ambition can produce a genuine natural *aristoi*. It is almost needless to say, as Jaffa points out, the natural *aristoi* are not philosophers. They are rather practically wise statesmen. Philosophers never assert a right to rule and any such claims to rule based on wisdom would evidence "a sure sign of a lack of wisdom."[55]

Jaffa poses this simple challenge to Zuckert's reliance on Strauss's supposed support for the natural right to rule of the naturally superior. The recognition of equality is a necessary precondition for the identification of the kinds of inequality possessed by the natural *aristoi*. Jaffa argues that the "claims of equality and inequality—of democracy and aristocracy— are reconciled" by "social contract," "the necessarily unanimous agreement, whereby human beings, being equally free and independent, no one having authority over another are transformed into fellow citizens, each equally subject to a government with lawful authority over them all." Jaffa concludes that "the function of the Lockean social contract, as understood by Jefferson and Lincoln, and by Leo Strauss . . . does not justify the radical individualism imputed to the social contract, as in the writings of Thomas Hobbes."[56] It is utterly surprising that Zuckert seems convinced that *Natural Right and History* was Strauss's last word on the Declaration of Independence and, more importantly, he seems determined that the founders read Locke with the precision, skill, and penetration that only Strauss was able to bring to bear in his reading of Locke.

How Did the Founders Understand Locke?

Professor Steven B. Smith wrote that although Strauss accepted the standard view that Lockean ideas formed the "theoretical foundation of the new American republic," he also revealed an "irony" that could not have escaped his "attentive readers" that "Hobbes, not Locke, was the true founder of America."[57] Strauss was the first to discover Hobbes buried deep below the surface of Locke in the esoteric interstices of his writing. Smith does express some reservations as to whether the founders understood Locke as a Hobbian: "Strauss may have exhibited some reservations about the radical character of the American founding, suggesting that the founders might have been saved from the 'the theoretical radicalism of Lockean principles [by] Locke's own prudence [which] to some degree successfully disguised the nature of [his] radicalism by emphasizing his links with the past.[58] In other words, the exoteric Locke might have saved the American founders from the radical modernity of the esoteric—Hobbian—Locke. Smith rightly argues—as does Jaffa—that the founders did not read Locke the way Strauss did, as indeed no philosopher, as far as we know, ever read him with the care and precision that Strauss did. The exoteric Locke, Strauss wrote was "the most influential of all modern natural right teachers." The reason for this, Strauss says, was because "he was an eminently prudent man, and he reaped the reward of superior prudence: he was listened to by many people, and he wielded an extraordinarily great influence on men of affairs and on a large body of opinion." Locke's prudence, knowing when to speak and when not to speak, presented the world "with and unbroken tradition of perfect respectability that stretches from Socrates to Locke."[59] The exoteric Locke is dominated by the virtue of prudence, the political virtue *par excellence*, which seems to defy in this statement of Strauss's the distinction between ancients and moderns. Thus, Locke's public message seems to be directed at statesmen, *phronimoi*, who are engaged in making prudential decisions about politics. The concern of Smith and others, however, is that Locke's esoteric teaching of radical modernity is more powerful and corrosive and will eventually undermine the benign effects of the "perfect respectability" of his public or exoteric teaching. Professor Smith concludes that America's "fateful concessions to modernity regarding the role of rights, commerce, and technology" made it impossible to avoid the inevitable consequences of Locke's "deeper teaching."[60] The recovery of natural right in modernity thus seems to be impossible. The critique of historicism cannot succeed. For Smith, the headlong slide into radical modernity seems fated by events beyond the control of any practically wise statesmen.

Even though he believed the attempt failed, Smith disagreed with Zuckert's account of Strauss's opening remarks about the Declaration in *Natural Right and History*. He thinks it may have been an "overt teaching" suggesting "a recovery of the possibility of natural right. . . . The book sets out a kind of irredentist strategy for reappropriating an earlier phase of modernity as a prophylactic against the corrosive effects of Rousseau, Marx, and Nietzsche." "Indeed," Smith continues, "*Natural Right and History* is nothing if not an invitation to American readers to take seriously their political founding and the philosophic ideas that gave rise to it. The American founding represented the first wave of modernity in the fulness of its theoretical vigor and self-confidence. It is necessary to recover some of the confidence today through the critique of historicism."[61] Jaffa, of course, argues in *A New Birth of Freedom* and *Crisis of the Strauss Divided* that the American founding represented Aristotelian natural right rather than the "first wave of modernity." But it is significant that Smith argues that Strauss is somehow inviting America to recover "the possibility of natural right," even though the forces of modernity will inevitably undermine the effort.

Michael and Catherine Zuckert in their collaborative book, *The Truth About Leo Strauss: Political Philosophy and American Democracy*, make one of the most incredible arguments ever encountered in the annals of serious scholarship. Jaffa had agreed with Smith (in part) that the founders had read the exoteric, not the esoteric (Hobbian) Locke. His argument was simple. Before Strauss, even the most accomplished political philosophers as far as anyone was aware were unable to penetrate to the esoteric depths as Strauss had to discover Locke's ultimate (if very carefully hidden) agreement with Hobbes and through Hobbes with Machiavelli. According to the Zuckerts "[a]s Jaffa sees it, the exoteric Locke is morally and political superior to the esoteric Locke; the founders' failure as philosophic readers was a fortunate thing."[62] "This line of argument remains problematic in several ways," the Zuckerts report: ". . . it seems to derogate from the honor due to the founders and Lincoln: they were not intelligent enough to grasp the real Locke and were saved from falling into dark modernity only by their stupidity." Well, of course, Jaffa never believed that the founders or Lincoln were stupid; but did he believe that they read Locke the way Strauss did, a way that no other philosopher did? These men were not philosophers, they were statesmen. They did not base their claim to rule on wisdom—no philosopher ever does, and anyone who does, as Strauss said innumerable times, is a fraud. To fault them because they didn't read Locke the way Strauss did seems nonsensical. Would the Zuckerts have been able to read Locke the way Strauss did without Strauss's guidance? They may flatter themselves; I may flatter myself. But I don't have the right to delude myself. In any case, the Zuckerts claim that even reading the exoteric Locke will lead you, will-thee-nil-thee, to the esoteric Locke. "To follow the exoteric Locke, according to Strauss, is to follow him a long way (if not quite all the way) to the conclusions of the esoteric Locke." Locke builds bridges to the orthodox, through Thomas Aquinas and Richard Hooker for example, but those bridges lead ultimately to Hobbes. All his bridges "are to lead the reader across into modern politics. That is what Strauss believed Locke succeeded in doing."[63] The point apparently is that you can't accept the exoteric Locke without getting the esoteric Locke whether you intend it or not. According to the Zuckerts that was Locke's grand scheme. Prudence had indeed been rendered superfluous by modernity and its adherents.

One of the reasons behind the Zuckerts' incredible opinion here might be that "in a post-Enlightenment environment" esoteric writing is no longer necessary, that the truth can stand on its own. In short, liberal democracy doesn't need secrets. Otherwise, why would Strauss reveal the secret of secret writing? Strauss said we faced a crisis of historicism that was leading ultimately to nihilism and the destruction of the civilized West. Historicism had obscured the idea of "esoteric" writing since it was a doctrine that believed that ideas were merely the product of each historical epoch and therefore irrelevant to subsequent epochs. The idea that there is anything like the possibility of eternal truths that could be communicated from one historical era to another, whether secretly or otherwise, was denied by historicism. Did this crisis—that esotericism would be forgotten—justify Strauss letting "the cat out of the bag" so to speak? Or did he really believe, as the Zuckerts think, that there was no longer any tension between philosophy and truth and society and orthodoxy? Strauss, of course, had to keep esotericism alive so that philosophers who were forced to practice the art in the pre-Enlightenment era could still be read and understood, but did he himself write esoterically? Or did he believe, along with the Zuckerts that it was no longer politically necessary?

The Zuckerts give an ambiguous answer. They do not believe that Strauss wrote esoterically, but they do believe that he deliberately made it difficult to understand his works. The reason, they believe, is that this would contribute to the "philosophic education" of his readers who would be forced "to work hard to piece out his conclusions;" this follows from the purely educational side of his enterprise. By writing difficult-to-understand books and what appear to be mere summaries, Strauss forces his readers to study the original texts on their own and thoroughly to ferret out his interpretative motives. The peculiar mode of writing that Strauss adopted in his later works no longer concerns persecution or noble lies, but only the effort to lead the young to what Strauss believed was a genuine education.[64] This description of Strauss's last works, sparse commentaries on esoteric works of philosophers hardly makes the Zuckerts' point. Strauss seems merely to be pushing the level of esotericism to a deeper level. These are commentaries written for future philosophers some of whom might have been young when Strauss wrote them. But Strauss's main concern in meeting the "crisis" of historicism was to preserve esotericism for the future, so that philosophy itself would survive the nihilism that will preside over the tyrannies of the future.

Anyone who believes that liberal democracy has dispensed with the need of speaking esoterically should merely look around today and judge for himself whether the truth can be spoken openly. The Zuckerts may reply that the United States is no longer a liberal democracy, or that while we march under the banner of liberal democracy, we are in fact a "seminary of intolerance." But is that not always the case? To think otherwise is simply to ignore what the study of the history of philosophy amply demonstrates and what the secret handshake between Thomas Aquinas and Thomas Jefferson confirms! Jefferson and Lincoln lived in the Age of Enlightenment and still found it necessary to dissemble in public, even though the law would not have punished them for their speech![65] But that "seminary of intolerance" would have kept them from being the outstanding Aristotelian statesmen they were had they not dissembled!

In 1948 Strauss wrote that "Tyranny is a danger coeval with political life." Tyranny is a potential wherever there is political life, whether in ancient or modern times. Strauss mentions that Xenophon's *Hiero* is "the only writing of the classical period which is explicitly devoted to the discussion of tyranny and its implications, and to nothing else, and which has never been subjected to comprehensive analysis."[66] Strauss's "comprehensive analysis" is a challenge for the most industrious student. It is a lesson on how to read a book that does not make its meaning available to the casual reader. But if "tyranny is a danger coeval with political life" and political life is indispensable to the human condition, does this mean that tyranny is a danger that defies the divide between ancients and moderns?

Strauss Revisits the Declaration of Independence in the City and Man

Professors Smith and Zuckert both make the same mistake: they believe that *Natural Right and History* was Strauss's last word on Locke (or a Hobbianized Locke) and the Declaration of Independence. It wasn't. Both Smith and Zuckert (and the Zuckerts) are unaware of an important passage near the center of *The City and Man* bearing on the Declaration. We know that Strauss rarely mentioned the Declaration; his most extensive discussion, although brief, occurs quite unexpectedly in the "Plato" chapter, published ten years after *Natural Right and History*:

> When the signers of the Declaration of Independence say: "we mutually pledge to each other our Lives, our Fortunes, and our sacred Honor," they mean that they are resolved to forsake their lives and fortunes, but to maintain their honor: honor shines most clearly when everything else is sacrificed for its sake, including life, the matter of the first natural right mentioned in the Declaration of Independence. While honor or justice

presupposes life and both are meant to serve life, they
are nevertheless higher in rank than life.[67]

Here Strauss clearly indicates that the authors of the Declaration ranked the goods of the soul higher than the goods
of the body by their willingness to sacrifice their natural
rights to life and property to "honor or justice." For Hobbes,
of course, courage is not a virtue, nor is honor any part of
the human good. It is utterly impossible to imagine Hobbes
ever pledging his "sacred honor" to any cause. This surely
means that in Strauss's final estimation, the founders were
not Hobbians, and if the orthodox Straussian view (including Zuckert's) is that Locke was in Strauss's estimation essentially (if secretly) a Hobbian, then by a parity of reasoning,
the Locke of *Natural Right and History* cannot be the Locke
of the American founding. Does this not provide proof that
Zuckert's dualities do not hold? That there may indeed be an
eidetic bridge after all between ancients and moderns that
is not imaginary. Was "the difference between ancients and
moderns" so "decisive" for Strauss after all?

There is one more example from *The City and Man* in
which I believe Jaffa shows that Strauss disputed modernity's claim to have banished prudence from the sphere of political life or that Machiavelli and his epigones had succeeded
in destroying the possibility of natural right. Our discussion
of Jaffa's "radical" position on these two issues, I say, are logical extensions of what appear to be changes Strauss made
since *Natural Right and History*, as our discussion of Strauss
on the Declaration above abundantly demonstrates. In any
case, Strauss remarks that

We cannot reasonably expect that a fresh understanding of classical political philosophy will supply us with

recipes for today's use. For the relative success of modern political philosophy has brought into being a kind of society wholly unknown to the classics, a kind of society to which the classical principles as stated and elaborated by the classics are not immediately applicable. Only we living today can possibly find a solution to the problems of today. But an adequate understanding of the principles as elaborated by the classics may be the indispensable starting point for an adequate analysis, to be achieved by us, of present-day society in its peculiar character, and for the wise application, to be achieved by us, of these principles to our tasks.[68]

An analysis "to be achieved by us" and a "wise application, to be achieved by us" is a description of Aristotelian natural right—classical wisdom applied to different political circumstances, even circumstances that may not have been in the contemplation of the classics. The repetition of the phrase "to be achieved by us" is striking. Classical prudence is available "for us" and is applicable to our situation as it is more or less applicable to all political situations. If Aristotle is correct that man is by nature a political animal, then natural right is a potential in every political community, depending upon circumstances and whether or not "enlightened statesmen" are present to recognize the potential and how it might best be applied to particular circumstances. We must remember that natural right, according to Aristotle, is a *part of political right* which everywhere has the same force or power (or dynamic, δύναμιν) but is everywhere changeable. It is prudence that rules the human world as such and that world is a political world. Prudence is both a moral and a practical virtue; it is the virtue of the statesmen, not of the philosopher. Jefferson,

Lincoln, and Jaffa believed that the founders were the *phronimoi* of Aristotle's *Nichomachean Ethics*. Based on this revealing passage from *The City and Man* I am inclined to agree and also inclined to agree that Jaffa's interpretation of prudence as being identical with natural right would be acceptable to Aristotle and Strauss.

Jaffa commented on the passage quoted above from the *The City and Man* in *Crisis of the Strauss Divided*: "The more I pondered these injunctions, the more convinced I became that this was precisely what the Founding Fathers had done some two centuries before. And to recapture what they had done—and what Lincoln had done in pursuit of their goals— was what our task was today. I was even more convinced that no advantage to public policy from the founders' achievement was possible until we had grasped that achievement. And for that we had to recapture the founders' Locke, which most certainly was not the Locke of *Natural Right and History*. I believe that in doing so, I was more faithful to Strauss's intention than those guardians of a Straussian orthodoxy who can 'learn nothing and forget nothing' in their insistence that modernity is bad and that America is modern."[69] Jaffa's judgment here is harsh, but we now know that Strauss in fact changed his mind about Locke and the American founding. *Natural Right and History* was not his last word on Locke or, if Jaffa's interpretation of the first paragraph of that book is correct, Strauss accepted Lincoln's view of natural right. If Strauss spoke in Lincoln's voice as his own, then he accepted Lincoln's view of natural right as expounded by Jaffa as authentic. This, of course, runs contrary to the "Straussian orthodoxy" that insists the divide between ancients and moderns can never be bridged in the manner that Jaffa suggested—or insisted.[70]

Jaffa comments on another passage from *The City and*

Man that provokes and even greater challenge to Straussian orthodoxy. Jaffa remarks that "One of the most emphatic expressions of Strauss's dedication to the central and unifying purpose of his life and work is in the beginning of *The City and Man*. . . . the first two paragraphs are extraordinary in their apparent difference from what both Professor Zuckert and I might think of as orthodox Straussianism." Jaffa quotes both paragraphs in full and comments on both. I will restrict myself to quoting only the second paragraph and commenting on Jaffa's interpretation of that paragraph. Strauss wrote:

> It is not sufficient for everyone to obey and to listen to the Divine Message of the City of Righteousness, the Faithful City. In order to propagate that message among the heathen, nay, in order to understand it as clearly and as fully as is humanly possible, one must also consider to what extent man could also discern the outlines of the City if left to himself, to the proper exercise of his own powers. But in our age it is much less urgent to show that political philosophy is the indispensable handmaid of theology than to show that political philosophy is the rightful queen of the social sciences, the sciences of man and of human affairs; even the highest law court in the land is more likely to defer to the contentions of social science than to the Ten Commandments as the words of the living God.

Jaffa calls the first sentence of this second paragraph "among the most astonishing Strauss, or perhaps anyone else in our time, ever wrote." "Notwithstanding the typographical eccentricity," Jaffa continues, "all of which is Strauss's," and is designed "to persuade us that he is speaking of Jerusalem," although "he never mentions it by name." "We would expect,"

Jaffa interjects, Strauss to argue "that the proper exercise of man's own unaided power would discern the outlines of Athens, not Jerusalem. Yet without a doubt 'that City' is one city, not two. This seems almost wantonly to negate the most fundamental of all the dualisms Zuckert attributes to Strauss, and which I am said to undermine."[71]

"The rest of the paragraph," Jaffa presses on, "is a single sentence, although it is divided by a semicolon which ought to have been a full stop." Jaffa calls the centerpiece of this single-sentence conclusion a "remarkable assertion." It is that "in our age it is much less urgent to show that political philosophy is the indispensable handmaid of theology." Jaffa concludes that this means that while it is "less urgent now" it does not mean that "there is no time at which it is not urgent." What is urgent now, Strauss indicates, is to demonstrate that "political philosophy" is the rightful queen of the social sciences, the sciences of human affairs." Jaffa helpfully informs us that the authoritative source for this is the first two chapters of the *Nicomachean Ethics*.

And, as Jaffa relates it, happiness contains "the idea that human life has a rational end or purpose, and that it can be ruled by reason, in great matters as in lesser ones. The highest end of human action is happiness, and the political philosopher is the architect of the structure of a life culminating in happiness."[72] Happiness, of course appears first in the Declaration "as a natural right of individuals, and then as the collective right of those same individuals joined by the social contract." Jaffa once again quotes George Washington that "there exists in the economy and course of nature and indissoluble union between virtue and happiness," commenting "it is difficult to imagine a more succinct or pithy Aristotelianism." "It is clear" Jaffa continues, "that for Washington

50

and for the *aristoi* here represented, the pursuit of happiness, both privately and politically, meant the pursuit of virtue. Political philosophy is accordingly the architecture of virtue as it leads to happiness. This is what Strauss meant by calling for its recognition as the queen of the social sciences. In the unity of the argument, all dualisms would seem to dissolve."[73]

Chapter Two

HARRY JAFFA DEFENDS COMPACT, STATESMANSHIP, AND THE RIGHT OF REVOLUTION

"[A]ll power in just & free Gov[ernmen]t is derived from compact."

—JAMES MADISON—
"Sovereignty"

*"The idea of compact is at the heart of American constitutionalism.
It is at the heart of the philosophical statesmanship that made
the Revolution, of which the Constitution is the fruit. In the most
fundamental respect, compact is an inference from the proposition
that 'all men are created equal.'"*

—HARRY JAFFA—
A New Birth of Freedom

Jaffa affirmed Madison's view that compact played an essential role in the American founding. In *A New Birth of Freedom*, he wrote in the most emphatic terms: "It is therefore of the highest importance that we understand the term 'compact' as an expression of the doctrine of the Declaration of Independence and as the essence of the philosophical and constitutional statesmanship of the Revolution." In fact, Jaffa wrote, compact was "ever present . . . to Americans of the Revolutionary generation" and "necessary . . . to their self-understanding."[1] Emphatic words, but hardly exaggerated. Jaffa was even more insistent when he revealed that both Madison and Lincoln believed that the Declaration of Independence *and the Constitution* were grounded in the right of revolution. We are accustomed to the argument that the Constitution serves as the means for securing the ends established in the Declaration. This was not, however, the view of the two principal authors of *Federalist*, the work that Jefferson in later years described as authoritative on "the general opinion of those who framed, and of those who accepted the Constitution."[2] Hamilton was a member of the founding generation and an influential (if unofficial) member of the Constitutional Convention who was committed—no less than Jefferson or Madison—to the revolutionary origins of America. Hamilton noted that that "[i]t has not a little contributed to the infirmities of the existing federal system that it never had a ratification by the PEOPLE. Resting on no better foundation than the consent of the several legislatures." Hamilton was anxious to counter the idea that convention ratification in the states could be used to "de-ratify" the Articles by the "right of legislative repeal." "However gross a heresy it may be to maintain," Hamilton continues, "that a *party* to a *compact* has a right to revoke that *compact*, the doctrine has itself had respectable advocates. The possibility of a question of this nature proves the necessity of laying the foundations of our national government deeper than in the mere sanction of delegated authority. The fabric of American empire ought to rest on the solid basis of THE CONSENT OF THE PEOPLE. The streams of national power ought to flow immediately from that pure, original fountain of all legitimate authority."[3] We, of course, won't vouch for the validity of Hamilton's opposition to compact based on "delegated authority." It was "heresy," and it had "respectable advocates" who *could* raise a *possible* question "*of this nature.*" It was to fend off these indistinct challenges that Hamilton takes up the cudgels that he wielded so well—the resort to first principles.

In *Federalist* 78, Hamilton defended a statement that Madison had made earlier in *Federalist* 40. Hamilton said: "I trust [that] the friends of the proposed Constitution will never concur with its enemies in questioning that fundamental principle of republican government which admits the right of the people to alter or abolish the established Constitution whenever they find it inconsistent with their happiness" (78:468). In *Federalist* 40, Madison had addressed the allegation that the Constitutional Convention had exceeded its authority. The Convention had been charged by the Confederation Congress with "the sole and express purpose of revising the articles of Confederation . . . [to] render the federal Constitution adequate to the exigencies of government and the preservation of the Union" (40:244). Madison, at his forensic best, argued that the instructions to the Convention were contradictory: no revision of the Articles could make them adequate precisely because the principles upon which the Articles rested were defective. It would therefore be of little avail to build a new structure on a defective foundation because the new superstructure would share in the deficiencies of the foundation itself. The real deficiency of the Articles was that it tried to create sovereign states within a sovereign union—as Hamilton described it in an earlier number of the *Federalist*, this was "a political monster" (15:103). Madison reasoned that a sound principle of legal construction required those who were faced with contradictory commands were obliged to choose the most important. It was obviously more important to have a constitution that was adequate to meet the exigencies facing the Union than one that was wholly inadequate but adhered strictly to the command that the Articles be revised.

Madison concluded that since "the plan to be framed and proposed was to be submitted to *the people themselves*, the disapprobation of the supreme authority would destroy it forever; its approbation blot out antecedent errors and irregularities" (40:249 emphasis original). In thus submitting the proposed constitution directly to the people, the Convention also subverted its charge to present the revisions to the Confederation Congress, which would, upon its approval, send them to the state legislatures, where a unanimous concurrence was required under the Articles for ratification. Madison and the leading Federalists, of course, knew that the Constitution as it emerged from the Convention would never be approved by the procedures established under the Articles because of its revolutionary innovations, not the least of which was ratification by the people rather than by state legislatures.

Madison was therefore forced to launch his boldest argument: "the establishment of a government adequate to the national happiness was the end at which [the Articles of Confederation] originally aimed, and to which they ought, as insufficient means, to have been sacrificed" (40:245). Lest there any doubt about the revolutionary character of the Convention's decision, the argument of *Federalist* 40 is even more explicit: "Let us view the ground on which the convention stood," Madison counsels. "It may be collected from their proceedings that they were deeply and unanimously impressed with the crisis, which had led their country almost with one voice to make so singular and solemn an experiment for correcting the errors of a system by which this crisis had been produced." Continuing in this aggressive vein, Madison asserts, as an ever-attentive witness to events in the Convention, the members of the Convention "must have reflected that in great changes of established government forms ought to give way to substance; that a rigid adherence in such cases to the forms would render nominal and nugatory the transcendent and precious right of the people to '**abolish or alter their governments** as to them shall seem most likely to effect their safety and happiness'" (40:249 [emphasis original]). A footnote indicates that the quotation was from the "Declaration of Independence." What is not noted is that the words "abolish" and "alter" have been transposed from the original which reads the people have the natural right to "alter or abolish" government and "provide new Guards for their future security."

It is clear, then, that the intention of the Convention was to "abolish" the Articles and not "alter" them. It was the natural right of self-preservation, authorized by the laws of nature and nature's God, that authorized "some *informal and unauthorized propositions*, made by some patriotic and respectable citizen or number of citizens. . . since it is impossible," Madison almost needlessly adds, "for the people spontaneously and universally to move in concert toward their object (40:248, 249 [emphasis original]). It should be remembered, of course, that these "respectable citizens," however much their proposals for a new constitution were "unauthorized," were not themselves "unauthorized," having been elected to the Convention by the people.

In the central number, *Federalist* No. 43, Madison asks

"[t]wo questions of a very delicate nature." The first is "on what principle" can "the Confederation, which stands in the solemn form of a compact among the States" be "superseded without the unanimous consent of the parties to it?" The answer Madison gives is the same one that we have already seen Hamilton give in *Federalist* 22, although in a less equivocal way. Again, Madison invokes the Declaration and the natural right to revolution. The question is answered, Madison responds, "by recurring to the absolute necessity of the case; to the great principle of self-preservation: to the transcendent law of nature and nature's God, which declares that the safety and happiness of society are the objects at which all political institutions aim and to which all such institutions must be sacrificed" (43:276). The Articles rest on nothing more than the positive or conventional principles of legislative approval. According to these principles, the approval of all members of the compact is not necessary for dissolution, because the violation of only one member can trigger dissolution. There are no natural law principles involved that would support the natural right to revolution or the invocation of the natural right of self-preservation in the case where the compact is supported merely by positive law. The multiple violations of state obligations under the Articles of Confederation were enough to invalidate ordinary obligations of compact, and these have happened without the permission of all thirteen members.

Chapter Two

Jaffa Comments on a Question of a "Very Delicate Nature"

Harry Jaffa comments on this first question of a "very delicate nature" and the role of the threat of revolution in elections. It is a theme that we have seen Jaffa explore before. "The threat or menace of revolution," Jaffa remarks,

> remains an integral element of the pressure brought to
> bear in and through the electoral process. That threat or
> menace, however, consists less in the fear of the force
> that might be brought to bear than in the reminder of
> the role of the right of revolution in the theory on which
> the American Revolution was grounded. . . . The appeal
> by the *Federalist* for the adoption of the Constitution of
> 1787 is in part an appeal to the law of nature against
> the positive law of the then existing constitution, the Ar-
> ticles of Confederation. The *Federalist* itself appears as
> campaign literature in an electoral process, the process
> of ratification, and as such was meant to produce only
> an effect on opinion, by exciting reflection. Its appeal to
> the right of revolution is purely peaceful and rational.
> Madison in the *Federalist* legitimates subsequent ap-
> peals, such as those in the Kentucky and Virginia Res-
> olutions, against the very government whose adoption
> he is recommending. These appeals are at once revolu-
> tionary, threatening, peaceful, and rational. The natural
> right of revolution, we may say, is the right whose recog-
> nition and understanding are supremely necessary if "re-
> flection and choice" are to replace "accident and force"
> in the government of mankind. The appeals to this right
> in 1798 were laying a foundation for an unprecedented
> transfer by free election.[4]

This must surely be one of the most remarkable passages in Harry Jaffa's entire corpus. The right of revolution which must always be present in the minds of voters is not primarily to render those who hold offices in government fearful, but to make them rational agents of "reflection and choice," which is the essential ground for rule by the consent of the governed. It is also the ground for constitutional government and the rule of law. But, according to Jaffa, the right of revolution—the ultimate expression of the people's sovereignty—understood in this manner also necessarily contains a degree of ambiguity.

1798 refers, of course, to the Virginia and Kentucky Resolutions which, Jaffa argues, "facilitated the process of majority consensus. This laid the groundwork for all future and free elections. On the other hand, by attributing to the opposition a design of despotism similar to the one that the Declaration of Independence had attributed to the British king and Parliament, the resolutions left open the inference that the people's sovereignty, expressed in and by their organization in states, might be exercised in revolutionary resistance rather than electoral change. This ambiguity," Jaffa concludes, "in the legacy of the resolutions explains why, at one and the same time, they laid the foundation for peaceful change by national elections and furnished arguments that justified rejecting the results of these elections."[5] We will quote Jaffa's statement below that the election of 1800 which may well have resulted from the 1798 Resolutions was the first election in history that witnessed the peaceful transfer of power based on the election of the people. Ballots may have replaced bullets in that election, but bullets always remained an important part of the self-consciousness of the people who went to the polls, both in their potential as revolutionaries and—if Jaffa is correct—for their deliberations as a people.

In 1835, James Madison was faced with the same regime questions that confronted Abraham Lincoln and Stephen A. Douglas, who, as we have seen, had become the acolyte of John C. Calhoun. Sometime in 1835, scarcely a year before his death, Madison addressed the dangerous crisis that was brewing over issues that had begun with the South Carolina Nullification Crisis. Madison was worried that his own efforts in 1800 were being misused to support arguments for nullification as a way of protecting minority rights; this would in later years transmogrify itself into arguments for a constitutional right to secession.[6] Madison primarily wanted to reaffirm the arguments he had vigorously made for ratification of the Constitution. Calhoun, of course, was the force behind the Nullification crisis that would ultimately become the crisis that precipitated the Civil War.

On December 11, 1787, *Federalist* twenty was published, written by Madison, with the assistance of Alexander Hamilton. In that number, the authors wrote that the "important truth . . . is that a sovereignty over sovereigns, a government over governments, a legislation for communities, as contradistinguished from individuals, as it is a solecism in theory, so in practice it is subversive of the order and ends of civil polity, by substituting *violence* in place of the mild and salutary *coercion* of the *magistracy*." (20:133–34 [emphasis original]).

A letter that Thomas Jefferson wrote from Paris to Edward Carrington carrying the date of August 4, 1787, provided an example of how "coercion" might easily replace "magistracy." The letter obviously did not arrive before the appearance of the *Federalist* number on December 11, but it does show that the three men were thinking alike and that Jefferson, a friendly critic of Confederation as a form of government, was able to express his opinions more freely in a private letter.

Speaking of the information he had received about the activities of the Convention, Jefferson comments: "My general plan would be, to make the States one as to everything connected with foreign nations, and several as to everything purely domestic." The "greatest defect" of the Articles of Confederation, Jefferson continues,

> is the imperfect manner in which matters of commerce have been provided for. It has been so often said, as to be generally believed, that Congress have no power by the Confederation to enforce anything; for example contributions of money. It was not necessary to give them that power expressly; they have it by the law of nature. When two parties make a compact, there results to each a power of compelling the other to execute it. Compulsion was never so easy as in our case, where a single frigate would soon levy on the commerce of any State the deficiency of the contributions; nor more safe than in the hands of Congress, which has always shown that it would wait, as it ought to do, to the last extremities, before it would execute any of its powers which are disagreeable.[7]

This last remark is written as playful irony since Jefferson's point throughout is that Congress is incapable of acting "to enforce anything." Jefferson notes that the Confederation Congress has no express power to enforce fiscal contributions. But Jefferson argues that express power is unnecessary because Congress has power under the "law of nature," meaning, the law of self-preservation. This would, of course, be a resort to natural right, the right of revolution.

The right of revolution—the ultimate expression of the people's sovereignty in a republic based on social compact— was never very far from the consciousness of the American constitution-makers.[8] Perhaps this should remind us of something that should always be in the forefront of the consciousness of republican citizens, even today: free elections are only possible as long as the natural right to revolution is remembered. Harry Jaffa wrote that "[n]ot until his inaugural address in 1801 would Jefferson see the right of free election as the normal and peaceable fruit of the right of revolution. But by Jefferson's theory, the right of revolution would forever underlie the right of free election and would supply a compelling reason why governments ought to have such elections as authentic expressions, not only of the people's will, but also of those rights that are the authority for the people's will. That is to say, the wholesome fear of the people by governments would also be a wholesome fear informing the majority in its dealings with minorities."[9]

When the South refused to accept the results of the election in 1860, bullets succeeded ballots, despite Lincoln's best efforts. Lincoln rightly refused to call the South's intransigence a revolution because it was not based on natural right principles, despite a variety of weak and ineffective attempts of some Southern states to invoke the principles of the Declaration.

Madison on Social Compact: The Limits on the Majority and the Rights of Conscience

What is most surprising about the "Sovereignty" essay is Madison's extended discussion of social compact which has no exact counterpart in the *Federalist*. The question of whether there can be a constitutional right to secession—the "ingenious sophism" as Lincoln would later call it—Madison avers, must be settled by the theory of social compact. Madison confirms Lincoln's characterization that the American Revolution did not dissolve "the social compact within the Colonies." Rather, the Colonies, he insists, achieved their independence as "United Colonies."[10]

Madison's statement about the central principle of compact deserves emphasis because it is categorical: "*all* power in *just* and *free* government is derived from compact." This, of course, reminds us of the statement in the Declaration that the "just powers" of government are derived from "the consent of the governed." We thus learn that "consent" authorizes only the "just powers," of government, not *all* powers of government. Consent must therefore conform to the requirements of "justice" as dictated by the "laws of nature and nature's God." In the "Sovereignty" essay Madison says that compact creates Government, but "arms it not only with a moral power, but the physical means of executing it." The "nature and extent of the powers" of the "compact itself" specifies "the obligations imposed on the parties to it." Compact thus exists to protect the rights and liberties—the "safety and happiness"—of those who consent, but it also creates moral obligations as well.[11]

The compact, Madison avers, is composed of individuals who agree to form civil society; this initial agreement requires unanimous consent, since no one can be ruled without his consent. This is an irrefragable dictate of the "laws of nature and nature's God," the foundation of which is the "self-evident truth" that "all men are created equal." Once they do so, however, unanimity cannot be expected for the administration of civil society; it must be administered by majority rule as a "plenary substitute for unanimity."

> Whatever by the hypothesis of the origin of the *lex majoris partis*, it is evident that it operates as a plenary substitute

of the will of the majority of the society for the will of the whole society; and that sovereignty of the society as vested in exercisable by the majority, may do anything that could be *rightfully* done by the unanimous concurrence of the members; the reserved rights of individuals (of conscience for example) in becoming parties to the original compact being beyond the legitimate reach of sovereignty, wherever vested or however viewed.[12]

Majority rule is a necessary substitute for unanimous consent. But even unanimous consent has limitations: it can do only what "could be *rightfully* done." "Rightfully" is undoubtedly used here to mean "justly." It would be unjust, for example, for the majority, even acting as the plenary substitute for *unanimous* consent, to invade the "reserved rights of individuals," which are always "beyond the legitimate reach of sovereignty, wherever vested or however viewed." Madison gives only one example of the "reserved rights of individuals"—the rights of "conscience." This was beyond the reach of sovereign power of any kind. Although not mentioned in the Declaration, the rights of conscience, Harry Jaffa wrote— the idea that "Almighty God hath created the mind free"— was the "most fundamental of the assumptions underlying the American political tradition."[13] It is the metaphysical freedom of the human mind—God's creation—that makes political freedom possible. The rights of conscience are the political expression of that metaphysical freedom. Jaffa begins to develop here his understanding of the theological-political question he will extend and deepen in his last publications. Social compact provides the basis for understanding this question. Jaffa's commentary on paragraph thirty-three of Lincoln's First Inaugural will be useful in its proper context.

Aristotle and Statesmanship

The relation between majority and minority would always remain a problem in republics and some solution had to be found for the protection of individual and minority rights, otherwise republican government could never claim to be non-despotic. Republican government based on the principle of equality held out the prospect of offering a coherent solution, but it would be an experiment without precedent. Without precedent, some unexpected fundamental regime questions were bound to arise. If we are to believe with Aristotle that human beings are by nature political and social animals, as Jaffa came to believe in his last publications that the founders did follow Aristotle on this fundamental principle, then natural right is always a part of every political regime. Depending on the character of the people and their circumstances, both moral and political, and whether philosophically wise statesmen—Aristotle's *phronimoi*—are present in the regime, natural right can be incorporated into the principles of the regime. By an almost providential confluence of events, all the necessary elements for a natural right founding were present in America.

The Constitution, Social Compact, Revolution and Zuckert Again

We have to bear in mind throughout Jaffa's discovery that the Constitution shares the same revolutionary grounds as the Declaration of Independence and received the same approval from the ultimate source of legitimate authority, ratification

66

by the people. The Constitutional Convention, we remember, violated its instructions to "reform the Articles," submitting instead an entirely new constitution to be approved by the supreme authority of the people; this amounted to a revolution based on the same principles of the "Laws of Nature and of Nature's God" that authorized the Declaration of Independence. Both documents therefore owe their natural right origins to social compact, the central principle of the Declaration of Independence. We mention here that Professor Michael Zuckert, discussed prominently in the previous chapter, denies that the founders relied on social compact or, if they did, he suggests it was a massive concession to the "low but solid" modernity of the founding. Zuckert's main complaint about social compact and the founding stems from his rejection of the principles of the Declaration of Independence which Washington, Jefferson, Hamilton, Madison, Lincoln, and Jaffa unequivocally agree rests on social compact and natural right.[14]

Jefferson, the Right of Revolution, and Lincoln

The central concept that forms the backdrop of *A New Birth of Freedom* is the right of revolution. "Abraham Lincoln," Jaffa says, "looked to Jefferson more than to anyone else for his understanding of the American Revolution."[15] Writing in the *Summary View of the Right of British America* in 1774, Jefferson, Jaffa explains, wrote in the Whig tradition that assumed that the "natural right of revolution" was legitimate. Jefferson referred to the natural right of emigration, which he described as the right "of departing from the country in which chance, not choice, has placed them," and removing to a place to live "under such laws and regulations as to them shall seem most likely to promote public happiness." Chance is merely "accident and force," whereas "choice" implies reason and natural right. Jaffa rightly comments that "[h]appiness is the objective good, and therefore the rational good, at which all laws and institutions aim. This is assumed by Jefferson, here and elsewhere, no less than by Aristotle, as it was by American public opinion of the Revolutionary generation."[16] Jaffa seems here to be starting his reevaluation of Aristotle's presence in the American founding which he will develop in detail in his last book, *Crisis of the Strauss Divided*.

Much of Jaffa's discussion of social compact is in the context of his refutation of John C. Calhoun's argument for the constitutionality of secession and states' rights. Since the main goal of this book is the attempt to comment on the Gettysburg Address and the Second Inaugural, I think that Jaffa's extended analysis of the First Inaugural is more suitable for that purpose. His commentary on that speech exhibits something unique in his writings; it is the only time he has numbered the paragraphs in a commentary. As it turns out, the numbering is quite helpful, and not just for keeping track of the argument.

Jaffa Comments on Lincoln's First Inaugural Address

After announcing he is ready to turn to the text of the Inaugural, Jaffa says he cannot "forbear mentioning" that this is exactly the speech that we would expect the author of the Lyceum Speech to give. In 1838 Lincoln had warned of the "growing tendency of lawlessness" and had advocated "reverence for the Constitution and the laws." Now the constitutionally chosen president will say why reverence for the Constitution and the laws is the only "guide to safety in the greatest crisis." Jaffa continues his "prelude" to the Inaugural with what seems, at first glance to be mere hyperbole: "No political leader in all human history began his office in the midst of more profound difficulties nor a situation in which his leadership depended upon such contrary imperatives. . . . No other political speech in history combines the timeless and the transient in such a delicate equilibrium. In the balance between the necessities of action and of thought, of the imperatives of the time and of the timeless, it has no superior and perhaps no equal." High praise indeed. But can anyone say that this is simply hyperbole? Or, if so, that it is unjustified?

Lincoln begins the First Inaugural with "In compliance with a custom as old as the government itself . . ." Jaffa remarks that "Lincoln combines 'custom' and 'old' in his first sentence, reminding us of the presumption of mankind of identifying the ancestral and the good, *a presumption to which unqualified assent can never be given*" (emphasis added).[17] Jaffa notes that everything that had been accepted as "ancestral truth" before the new order introduced by the American Revolution was rejected. The heart of the *novus ordo seclorum*, Jaffa claims, was the fact the "[n]o constitution before that of 1787 had ever prohibited a religious test for office" and "[n]o head of state before President Washington in 1790 had ever addressed Jews as equal fellow citizens." Thus, it seems that the American Revolution was a theological-political revolution grounded in freedom of conscience. I say, then, that the theological-political question is for Jaffa and Lincoln the central question of social compact. Once natural right emerges, it is indispensable to adapt it to the regnant theology or, if necessary, to make efforts to restore the regnant theology.

I made a somewhat different interpretation of the opening line of the First Inaugural at the beginning of chapter five that, while different, does not disagree with Jaffa's interpretation here. Jaffa concludes by observing Lincoln's rhetorical turn: "Lincoln defers to *wise* custom. How wise," Jaffa continues, "we will learn only later, when Lincoln turns the oath of office into a powerful means of preserving the very Constitution that enjoins the oath upon him" (emphasis original).

In paragraphs two, three, and four, Lincoln assures the people of the Southern states that he has no intention or inclination or "lawful right" to interfere with slavery where it already exists. But Jaffa rightly notes that the South most often pointed to the text of the House Divided speech where Lincoln expressed his determined opinion that the Constitution had put slavery on the course of ultimate extinction as the greatest danger to their peculiar institution that was occasioned by his election. Beginning with the Peoria Speech in 1854 Lincoln used the Declaration as the focal point of his attack on Douglas and the Democrats. By the time of the First Inaugural, he had begun to downplay his reliance on the purely rational *principles* of the Declaration and turned to emphasizing its status as "our *ancient faith*." Lincoln probably calculated that this strategy would have a greater appeal to Southern churches, already beginning to read biblical texts in support of slavery.[18]

Jaffa brings up the issue of the Republican Guarantee Clause, which was part of the slavery debate in the 1850s and 1860s but is not a subject clearly raised in paragraphs four and five. When the Republican Guarantee Clause was added to the Constitution six states permitted slavery. There was no substantive discussion at the Constitutional Convention about what constituted Republican government and John C. Calhoun's argument always was that since slave states were accepted into the Union slavery was obviously compatible with the "Republican Guarantee" requirement. But, of course, it is difficult to square the idea that republican government which, in Lincoln's view, must be derived from the consent of *all* the governed, can ever tolerate slavery. We discussed in the last chapter, the moral limits that the "Laws of Nature and Nature's God" places on majority rule. As Jaffa remarks, in his analysis of the First Inaugural, "[i]t was clear to Lincoln, although not so clear to many of his contemporaries, that the 'consent of the governed' could be rightfully exercised only within the boundaries of the moral law that gives consent its validity but whose validity does not depend upon consent." "If the republican form of government is based upon the consent of the governed," Jaffa contends,

> as the seceding Southerners themselves insisted, how could the government of slaves be consistent with republicanism? How could anyone demand to be governed only with his own consent while denying to others even the slightest semblance of that right?[19]

This argument, putatively about the republican form of government, tracks the Declaration's case for equality and consent. The argument for equality and consent would hardly be convincing to Southern intransigence in 1861, but the South might possibly listen if the Declaration was used to defend the Republican Guarantee clause and an entirely new argument for federalism was drawn from the Declaration that would benefit the South.

Jaffa brashly remarks,

> if the United States guaranteed a republican form of government to each of the states, and if fifteen of the

states receiving that guarantee had slavery among their domestic institutions, did not that necessarily imply it was a republican institution?

Jaffa continues by remarking that Article IV also extends "protection due to each state 'against domestic violence'" which was widely understood to include slave rebellions as well as other kinds of unlawful uprisings.[20]

Jaffa traces "the principles of American federalism" to its ground "in the Declaration of Independence" which "requires that the ordinary police powers of government reside in the states and in their localities, and not in the federal government. That is to say," Jaffa seems to clarify, "the 'laws of nature and of nature's God,' must be entrusted to political authorities immediately responsible to those whose lives and property are to be protected." It is not obvious that the Declaration endorses this precise version of federalism, but it might be supposed that if all legitimate power is derived from the consent of the governed, then government should be closest to those upon whose consent it rests. Jaffa states the general principle that might be mandated by the Declaration: "This means not only that the police power resides in the states rather than in the federal government but also that the states themselves delegate a necessary and sufficient portion of that power to local authorities responsible to the communities they serve." Presumably the prudence of wise legislators will determine the precise configuration of the local communities, and the police powers allotted to them. "It is in the same sense *according to nature*," Jaffa continues, "that only the federal government can provide security to the Union as a whole against external dangers and that the federal government cannot provide security to individual communities within the Union." "Majority rule," thus "has its natural limits." A national majority cannot decide for a state or a local community, Jaffa argues:

> Lincoln did not expect the responsibility for the security of a Southern town, any more than that of a Northern town, to be placed anywhere but in the hands of the townsmen themselves. The government of the slaves was looked upon as a matter of security by Southerners. Whether they ought to have looked upon it as they did, the principles of the Declaration made it a matter of right, and not only of prudence, that those immediately concerned be the rightful judges of what constituted their own security. Thus Lincoln was not merely abiding by a constitutional compromise when he said that he had no inclination to interfere with slavery in states where it was lawful.

When Lincoln said in the First Inaugural that he had no "lawful power" or "inclination" to interfere with slavery in the states where it already existed, the casual reader—myself included—always assumed he meant that he was adhering to the compromises of Constitution. If Jaffa is correct that the scheme of federalism dividing national from state and local powers is a dictate of natural law, then state power over slavery is not merely a matter of constitutional compromise or the prudence that arises from compromise but emanates from the laws of nature and nature's God. From Jaffa's account, state control over slavery is supported by the Declaration.

As we mentioned above, a point that needs repeating, Lincoln, even before the First Inaugural, had begun to deemphasize his reliance on the Declaration, emphasizing instead "our ancient faith" as a more palatable phrase for Southern ears. Jaffa's efforts to interpret the Declaration here are not Lincoln's—but they are a much more sophisticated adumbration—of how the Declaration extends to questions of social compact and political rhetoric.

In paragraphs five and six, Lincoln addresses the federal question in the context of the fugitive slave clause, this time exclusively as a constitutional issue. Lincoln says that the fugitive slave clause is "as plainly written in Constitution as any other of its provisions." After Lincoln quotes the provision in the Constitution, he comments that "[i]t is scarcely to be questioned that this provision was intended by those who made it, for the reclaiming of what we call fugitive slaves . . ." Here Lincoln adds this remarkable phrase: "and the intention of the law-giver is the law." This perfectly Aristotelian idea supports Lincoln's concept of original intent jurisprudence. But Lincoln uses it here, not so much to prove his fidelity to the fugitive slave clause or to support the right of each state to control its own domestic institutions, but as Jaffa mentions, to prepare the ground, in paragraph eight, to request legislation for the better protection of free slaves against slave catchers. In paragraph seven Lincoln seemed utterly indifferent to the federal question, remarking that "[t]here is some difference of opinion whether this clause should be enforced by national or by state authority; but surely that difference is not a very material one. If the slave is to be surrendered, it can be of little consequence to him, or to others, by which authority it is done."

The indifference of paragraph seven serves as a prelude to a plea for a liberalized protection for free slaves: "ought not all the safeguards of liberty known in civilized and humane jurisprudence to be introduced, so that a free man be not, in any case, surrendered as a slave?" This law, Lincoln advocated, is justified by the Privileges and Immunities Clause of Article IV of the Constitution. If Jaffa is right—as I believe he is—that Lincoln agreed, following the arguments of Jefferson, Hamilton, and Madison described in the previous chapter—that the Constitution rested on the same principles of the laws of nature as the Declaration, then the rights guaranteed by the Privileges and Immunities clause were derived directly from the principles of natural right. This was an argument that was frequently made by Republicans in the thirty-ninth congress and was also Abraham Lincoln's vision that was ultimately embodied in the first section of the Fourteenth Amendment.[21]

Whether the Privileges and Immunities clause was intended to apply to blacks of African descent was a matter of special concern to Chief Justice Taney in the *Dred Scott* case. In his opinion for the Court, he argued that the Declaration and Constitution were never intended to include blacks of African descent—whether free or slave—as part of the people who "framed and ratified the Constitution" and they therefore could not be considered citizens of the United States. Under the Privileges and Immunities clause of Article IV, however, free blacks who were citizens of states would be automatically accorded all the rights and privileges of state citizens in the States. In an argument that reads almost like a cruel parody, Taney remarks that "[i]f persons of the African race are citizens of a State, and of the United States they would be entitled to all of these privileges and immunities in every State, and the State could not restrict them for they would hold these privileges and immunities under the paramount authority of the Federal Government." Federal courts, Taney maintained, would be obliged to enforce these rights, the laws and constitutions of the States to the contrary notwithstanding. The Privileges and Immunities Clause, Taney concluded, "guaranties rights to the citizen, and the State cannot withhold them." This interpretation of Article IV, up to this point, seems eminently correct, but Taney used it to reach a fantastic conclusion: free blacks would be citizens and given federal protection for their rights in all the States. This would lead to unwonted "consequences" in the slave States where the rights of blacks would be enforced by the Federal government.[22] Taney implies that none of the southern delegates to the Constitutional Convention would have agreed to this—unless they understood that blacks of African descent, free or slave, could never be citizens of the United States or a State because they were no part of the people described in the Declaration or any part of "We the people" who framed and ratified the Constitution *or* there was an understanding that the Constitution gave the Federal government no power to enforce the provisions of Article IV.

The Chief Justice was banking on the latter proposition. We have the testimony of John H. Bingham, who introduced the first draft of the section one of the Fourteenth Amendment before the House on Feb. 26, 1866: "The Congress shall have power to make all laws which shall be necessary and proper to secure to the citizens of each state all privileges and immunities of citizens in the several states." Why did Bingham think this was an urgent necessity? Bingham argued that it was a defect of the original Constitution that there was no express grant of power to Congress to enforce the provisions of the Privileges and Immunities clause of Article IV. The rights protected in the "immortal bill of rights" are, Bingham asserted, fundamental privileges and immunities possessed by the citizens of the United States, but those essential rights, he continued, as

embodied in the Constitution, rested for [their] execu-
tion and enforcement hitherto upon the fidelity of the
States. The House knows, the country knows, the civilized world knows, that the legislative, executive, and
judicial officers of eleven States within this Union within
the last five years, in utter disregard of these injunction
of your Constitution, in utter disregard of that official
oath which the Constitution required they should sev-
erally take and faithfully keep when they entered upon
the discharge of their respective duties, have violated in
every sense of the word these provisions of the Constitution of the United States, the enforcement of which are
absolutely essential to American nationality.[23]

The final version of section one of the Amendment was not,
of course, based on Bingham's first proposal, but was a prohibition against any state making or enforcing any "law which
shall abridge the privileges or immunities of citizens of the
United States" and did make its way in the language of the
Fourteenth Amendment. Indeed, Bingham deserves the lion's
share of credit for the language of the first section, with the
exception of the first sentence defining citizenship. As Bingham himself remarked in debate in the House in 1871: "I had
the honor to frame . . . the first section [of the Fourteenth
Amendment] as it now stands, letter for letter and syllable for
syllable . . . save for the introductory clause defining citizens."[24]

In paragraph nine, Lincoln says he takes the oath of office "with no mental reservations," and has "no purpose
to construe the Constitution or laws, by any hypercritical
rules." In other words, as Jaffa comments, Lincoln "is saying
quite plainly. . . that he will interpret the Constitution and
laws plainly and will not, by clever interpretations, discover

meanings in them that any ordinary citizen would not recognize."[25] Lincoln proceeds to announce, however, that it may be proper not to enforce all the laws, especially, as we learn later in the speech, where enforcing some laws may lead to bloodshed. What is surprising is the fact that this announcement follows the paragraph on the "Privileges and Immunities" clause, where the Federal government's lack of enforcement, if Bingham was correct, sowed the seeds of Civil War at the founding itself. [26] In paragraph one Lincoln had referred to his oath-taking as a "custom;" here in paragraph nine, it is the "official oath."

Paragraphs ten and eleven address the right of revolution, and the perpetuity of the Union. These are themes that we have previously examined *in extenso*. Lincoln set the unique stage for his discussion: in all previous inaugurations, a disruption of the Union was "only menaced, it is now formidably attempted." Jaffa repeats the thesis that is pervasive in *A New Birth of Freedom*: "Can ballots in all cases succeed bullets as a means of preserving the people's rights? Was not the nation founded upon the exercise of the right of revolution?"[27] The South, of course, did not seriously appeal to the right of revolution, but rather to the Constitution as supporting a legal right to secession. Lincoln naturally argued that the Union was perpetual, that the Union was older than the States; the Union created the States, the States did not create the Union. We recall the argument of *Federalist* forty-three: the end or purpose of social compact was the "safety and happiness of the people", and all forms must be sacrificed to this purpose. A sovereignty consisting of sovereign states—a compact of states—is inadequate (a "solecism") to accomplish that purpose and must be sacrificed. The Constitution as approved by the only legitimate source of legitimate power, the sovereign people, rested on the principles of the law of nature as much as the Declaration of Independence and therefore had the same status as a founding document as the Declaration. The Constitution, as an "organic law," could not contain the means of its own dissolution; it cannot countenance the right to revolution in any form. Substance—ends or purpose—can never give way to forms. That is what the South demanded. Lincoln stands firm!

Jaffa comments on paragraphs thirteen, fourteen, and fifteen together, characterizing the three as a "history" in which Lincoln anticipates "the metaphor of the Gettysburg Address," the "prenatal history" of "the Union as a national government." The "prenatal history" begins with the famous "conceived in liberty" phrase of the Gettysburg Address which is said to have been consummated in 1774, and led to the birth in 1776. Jaffa comments that "Lincoln ignores the Confederate contention that in 1776 the thirteen states declared their independence of each other, as well as of Great Britain." He attributes this to the fact that the inaugural took place before Fort Sumter and there was still hope, however dubious, that Lincoln did not think it prudent to disappoint this proposition of his "dissatisfied fellow-countrymen." It was unquestionable that the Constitution, when submitted for ratification, would come into existence when ratified by the people of nine states. Unanimity was not a requirement. Yet, Lincoln could have easily argued that it was the people of the states, not the states themselves, who were ratifying the Constitution. This is undoubtedly the way Madison and Hamilton understood the matter—and so did Lincoln.

Lincoln declares in paragraph sixteen that the "in view of the Constitution and the laws, the Union is unbroken;" and pledges that "to the extent of my ability, I shall take care, as the Constitution itself expressly enjoins upon me, that the laws of the Union be faithfully executed in all the States." Lincoln continues that he deems this "to be only a simple duty on my part; and I shall perform it, so far as practicable, unless my rightful masters, the American people, shall withhold the requisite means, or, in some authoritative manner, direct the contrary. I trust," Lincoln concludes, "this will not be regarded as a menace, but only as the declared purpose of the Union that it will consti-tutionally defend and maintain itself." Jaffa contrasts this with President Buchannan's interpretation of the Constitu-tion that neither congress nor the president had the power to coerce the states into remaining in the Union. Lincoln, on the contrary, "declares that all resolves and ordinances of secession are legally void and the Union unbroken." Jaffa parses Lincoln's words to mean that "[s]ecession in name is rebellion in fact, and the constitutional power to sup-press rebellion was unquestionable." Jaffa asks, how could this not be a menace? "Rebellions or invasions," Jaffa rightly notes, "can be met only by armed force, and only Congress possessed the constitutional power to raise, support, and maintain armed forces."[28] The thirty-seventh congress was elected in November 1860 and ordinarily would go out of session in December, 1860 and not reconvene until Decem-ber, 1861. Jaffa remarks that "[t]o wait that long would be tantamount to abandoning the Union. When he delivered his inaugural, Lincoln did not even know what the compo-sition of the Congress would be."[29] Lincoln had said that his "rightful masters" were "the American people." But Jaffa asks the important question at this point: "In a nation as divided as the United States on the eve of the Civil War, who can qualify as *being* the people?"[30]

Jaffa considers paragraphs seventeen and eighteen together. Lincoln said in paragraph seventeen that "there needs to be no bloodshed or violence; and there shall be none, unless it be forced upon the national authority." Constitutional power conferred on the president, Lincoln said, "will be used to hold, occupy, and possess the property, and places belonging to the government, and to collect the duties and imposts; but beyond what may be necessary for these objects, there will be no invasion—no using of force against or among the people anywhere." Paragraph eighteen promises that the mails will be delivered "unless repelled," and "[s]o far as possible, the people everywhere shall have that sense of perfect security which is most favorable to calm thought and reflection." This course will be followed unless "current events, and experience" shall indicate "a modification or change to be proper" in which case "my best discretion will be exercised. . ." Jaffa highlights the ambiguities of Lincoln's paragraph. But the ambiguity hardly conceals the practical wisdom of the pronouncements. "Of course," Jaffa intones, "Lincoln would not, because he could not, enforce the laws where no enforcement mechanism existed. Of course he would not, because he could not, deliver the mails where they were repelled. The question remained: How could enforcement mechanisms be reinstated? And how could the repelling of the mails be itself repelled? In the end Lincoln answered these questions with the Union armies, and we assume with some confidence that, in his own mind, he already knew here that that would be necessary."[31] Since at the time of the Inaugural the Union army was virtually non-existent, and the composition of the Congress necessary to authorize its existence unknown to Lincoln, the tentative character of this extraordinary speech transmogrifies into remarkable boldness.

Jaffa also comments on paragraphs nineteen and twenty together. In paragraph nineteen, Lincoln remarks that he "will neither affirm or deny" the existence of "persons in one section, or another, who seek to destroy the Union at all events, and are glad of any pretext to do so." Lincoln says he "need address no word to them. To those who really love the Union, may I not speak?" In paragraph twenty he counsels caution but directed only "to those who really love the Union." Jaffa remarks that the message here will be repeated "again, most concisely, in the Gettysburg Address. Implicit in everything he says," Jaffa continues, "is the thesis that the benefits of a free society cannot be long enjoyed by those who would arbitrarily deny them to others. . . . Hence the underlying question remains: Can those for whom slavery is a 'positive good' or those who are indifferent to slavery love the Union as do those for whom the Union is the practical implementation of the human freedom embodied in the Declaration?"[32]

Jaffa comments on paragraph twenty-one separately. In this paragraph, Lincoln makes the simple assertion that "[a]ll profess to be content in the Union, if all constitutional rights can be maintained. Is it true, then, that any right, plainly written in the Constitution, has been denied? I think not. Happily the human mind is so constituted, that no party can reach to the audacity of doing this. Think, if you can, of a single instance in which a plainly written provision of the Constitution has ever been denied." Jaffa in his commentary queries: "Why does Lincoln make a hyperbolic assertion as that 'the human mind is so constituted' as to be incapable of 'the audacity' of denying that a 'plainly written' constitutional right has been denied? Lincoln knew perfectly well that there were no limits to the capacity of the human mind to deny what is true or affirm what is false. Clearly, he is bent upon impressing on his audience the distinction between what is plainly written and what is implied."[33] Jaffa doesn't mention it here, but Lincoln often ridiculed Taney's statement in his *Dred Scott* decision that "the right of property in a slave is distinctly and expressly affirmed in the Constitution."[34] Lincoln simply argued that the right of property in a slave could not possibly be "*distinctly and expressly* affirmed in the Constitution" because the words "slave" and "slavery" never appear in the text. But perhaps Taney believed it was a necessary inference from the text. The real question in terms of personal rights was whether a slave was a person or property. Under the terms of the Fifth Amendment "no person" can be "deprived of life, liberty, or property, without due process of law." The three times slaves are referred to in the Constitution, the word "persons" is used in these circumlocutions: "three-fifths of all other persons"; "the migration or importation of such persons'" "persons held to service or labor." Indeed, this was the principal debate throughout the 1850s: was a black of African descent a person or property. In terms of the Constitution, he was called a "person." But in other respects, slaves were treated as property, especially in the so-called fugitive slave clause, which, in effect, nationalized slavery; a tax was also allowed on the importation of slaves which clearly implied the status of slaves as property. So, in terms of the Fifth Amendment, if a black of African descent was a person, he was entitled to life, liberty and property; if property, then he belonged, as a chattel to a master. This was the issue that prepared civil war from the very beginning; it was the issue that made Jefferson, and later Lincoln, "tremble" for the fate of America, knowing that God's justice cannot sleep forever.

Jaffa deals with paragraphs twenty-two and twenty-three together. His commentary is noteworthy and describes Lincoln's Socratic-like dialectic with effusive hyperbole that is unusual even for this master of hyperbolic excess. "Never since Socrates," Jaffa claims,

> has philosophy so certainly descended from the heavens into the affairs of mortal men. While addressing the immediate crisis, Lincoln is delivering a lecture to all men and all times on the essentials of free government. He is, we are tempted to say, the eternal political science professor addressing the eternal class. Starting from his premises, the mathematical character of his reasoning leaves no options except the ones to which he points. Ironically, the coincidence of philosophy and political power that Lincoln here represents only serves to underlie the Platonic truth, which Lincoln learned from Shakespeare, that philosophy cannot cause the 'evil in the cities' to cease and that politics is the realm of the tragic. In the presence of Lincoln's arguments, no sane person would have opted, as the South did, for secession, slavery, and war. Lincoln knew when he spoke these lines that they would have no effect upon the actions or passions of his antagonists.[35]

Jaffa writes as if Lincoln were speaking lines from a Shakespearean play! There is no evidence the Lincoln ever read Plato (although he mentions him once), so it is quite reasonable to presume that he learned Platonic themes through the greatest Platonic poet ever to live. The theme of the "coincidence of philosophy and power" and "that politics is the realm of the tragic" Lincoln would have learned from Shakespeare; he would also have learned the limits of political rhetoric, that reason cannot persuade those held in thrall by their passions. What did Lincoln say that provoked such hyperbole from Harry Jaffa?

In paragraph twenty-two Lincoln makes something of a categorical statement. In paragraph twenty-one Lincoln had asked: "Is it true, then, that any right, plainly written in the Constitution, has been denied?" He now states that:

> From questions of this class spring all our constitutional controversies, and we divide upon them into majorities and minorities. If the minority will not acquiesce, the majority must, or the government must cease. There is no other alternative; for continuing the government, is acquiescence on the one side or the other. If a minority, in such case, will secede rather than acquiesce, they make a precedent which, in turn, will divide and ruin them; for a minority of their own will secede from them, whenever a majority refuses to be controlled by such a minority. . . . All who cherish disunion sentiments, are now being educated to the exact temper of doing this. Is there such a perfect identity of interests in the States to compose a new Union, as to produce harmony only, and prevent renewed secession?

We note first that questions of whether or not "plainly written" rights in the Constitution have been violated belong to a "class" of rights which presumably includes all rights in the Constitution. Does it contain rights that are necessarily inferable from plainly written rights? Madison in the essay on "Sovereignty," which in some sense must be considered authoritative, which was discussed above, but deserves to be briefly revisited here. Madison expressly argued that the final "exposition" of the Constitution belonged to the national government.[36] Madison was concerned, as Lincoln is here, with the limits of majority rule. He argued, we recall, that the "reserved rights of individuals" were beyond the reach of majorities, and he specified only the rights of conscience.[37] Madison knew, of course, that the rights of conscience were only inferable from the First Amendment or from the fact that Article VI forbids any religious test as a requirement for holding any office or public trust under the United States. Today, this would be called an unenumerated right. But if Jaffa is correct that the Constitution rests on the same ground of authority as the Declaration, then the Constitution has the same status in the law of nature. The rights of conscience belong to the laws of nature and nature's god and properly speaking are not inferable from the Constitution, but from the right of revolution.

In paragraph twenty-three, Lincoln answers his own rhetorical question. "Plainly, the central idea of secession, is the essence of anarchy." Anarchy, of course, cannot be a principle of rule as the very term itself suggests. The true principle of rule for republican government and a free people, as we have quoted before, is stated with a clarity and precision that the world had never heard before. If I possessed Jaffa's art of hyperbole, I would use employ it now, but I do not dare compete with the master. I need only quote Lincoln who is himself unsurpassed:

> A majority, held in restraint by constitutional checks and limitations, and always changing easily, with deliberate changes of popular opinions and sentiments, is the only true sovereign of a free people. Whoever rejects it, does, of necessity, fly to anarchy or to despotism. Unanimity is impossible; the rule of a minority, as a permanent arrangement, is wholly inadmissible; so that, rejecting the

majority principle, anarchy, or despotism in some form,
is all that is left.

Jaffa, of course, was correct when he stated that Lincoln spoke
with "mathematical" precision. But mathematics is not dialec-
tics, although it may share something with mathematics. But
most importantly, politics are not mathematics. Rhetoric is
closer to politics. As a matter of rhetoric, Lincoln left unstated his ultimate conclusion: "anarchy or despotism" is all that is
left. Unstated is the fact that anarchy is unsustainable; it always
ends in despotism. The state of nature, the "war of all against
all," drives both the strong and weak into the arms of Leviathan.

At this juncture, Harry Jaffa interrupts his paragraph-by-
paragraph commentary of the First Inaugural and engages
in what I will call an excursus that occupies the next fifty-
six pages of text to resume with commentary on paragraph
twenty-four. Most of this excursus involves "questions raised
by *Dred Scott*." "This case," Jaffa rightly contends, "represented a challenge" to Lincoln's statement in the First Inaugural
about the majority being the only "true sovereign" in republican government. "By definition," Jaffa says, "such a majority
operates within the boundaries of the Constitution, in which
the rights of the minorities are not placed at risk by the rule
of the majority." But as we have seen, Taney had declared
that the owner's right to carry his slave property into the territories was beyond the right of any constitutional majority
to deny.[38] We will not follow Jaffa on his excurses because an
extended discussion of *Dred Scott* will be presented in chapter three. We will take up the commentary as it resumes with
paragraph twenty-four.

Paragraph twenty-four is the much-discussed passage on
Lincoln's judicial thought. Lincoln begins by saying

> I do not forget the position assumed by some, that con-
> stitutional questions are to be decided by the Supreme
> Court; nor do I deny that such decisions must be binding
> in any case, upon the parties to the suit, as to the object
> of that suit, while they are also entitled to very high re-
> spect and consideration in all parallel cases by all other
> departments of the government.

Opinions can be overruled, or holdings limited to particular cases. But if public policy can be fixed irrevocably on vital questions by decisions of the Supreme Court affecting private parties in ordinary cases, then the people will have surrendered their sovereignty to the Supreme Court. This view, Lincoln concluded, does not imply "any assault upon the court or the judges. It is a duty from which they may not shrink, to decide cases properly before them; and is no fault of theirs if others seek to turn their decisions to political purposes."

Jaffa comments that "[t]he most striking thing about this paragraph, and in particular its ending, is how it differs from nearly everything Lincoln had said hitherto about *Dred Scott*. In the House Divided speech, Chief Justice Taney was portrayed as an active participant in a conspiracy to extend slavery nationwide."[39] Jaffa reaches the heart of the matter when he says that Lincoln's truism that the Supreme Court could make mistakes was epitomized by the one Taney made when he denied that blacks of African descent "had any rights that the white man was bound to respect. Consistent with this error was Taney's denial that the Declaration's proposition of human equality meant what it said. Here Taney was flatly denying the historical record and in the process was transforming American constitutionalism from its foundation in the 'laws of nature and of nature's God' to that of the right of the stronger."[40]

Paragraph twenty-five rehearses the moral question in these famous lines: "One section of our country believes slavery is *right*, and ought to be extended, while the other believes it is *wrong*, and ought not to be extended. This is the only substantial dispute." The constitutional question is ultimately the question of the morality of slavery, the question of the Declaration of Independence. There is no middle ground between natural right and positive right, positive right must be tested ultimately by natural right. The promise to obey the fugitive slave law and the law for suppressing the foreign slave trade which Lincoln makes in the rest of the paragraph in an attempt to appease the South will serve only to delay a final reckoning, even if the slaveocracy were willing to listen.

Paragraph twenty-six runs through a theme that Lincoln will repeat in later years. Physically speaking we cannot separate. We will remain face to face. Amicable relations will be better than hostile ones. Jaffa smartly recognizes that "the dominant theme in the remaining paragraphs, as it was in Jeffersons inaugural, is friendship as the basis of union. A subdominant theme," Jaffa reveals, "is the right of revolution, not as a threat to the Union, but as the basis of the friendship that formed the Union." Lincoln is pointing a low kind of utilitarian friendship, but most importantly Jaffa says, "it makes no assumption of moral superiority on one side or the other," although Jaffa is quick to point out that "Lincoln does not say anything here that implies a weakening of his resolve to end the extension of slavery." But there was a political and rhetorical calculus connected with the lack of any expression of "moral superiority." At the time Lincoln speaks, "there are still more slave states *in* the Union than *out* of it. The presence of loyal slave states, now and in the war to come, was vital to the success of the antislavery cause no less than to that of union."[41]

Jaffa comments on paragraphs twenty-seven and twenty-eight together. Paragraph twenty-seven is about constitutional change: amendment or revolution? Paragraph twenty-eight deals with an amendment that has been proposed prohibiting Congress from forbidding slavery in the states. Lincoln says he would recommend the Convention mode for amendment, allowing the people to select the delegates directly to recommend the language of the amendment. Jaffa in his commentary on these paragraphs says that "Lincoln is perfectly candid about the right of revolution, as indeed he must be, since at the center of everything he believes is [contained in] the Declaration of Independence." Jaffa mentions Lincoln's speech in the House in 1848 on the Mexican War where he spoke expansively on the right of revolution. "Any people anywhere," Lincoln said, "being inclined and having the power, have the right to rise up and shake off the existing government, and form a new one that suits them better. This is a most valuable, a most sacred right—a right which, we hope and believe, is to liberate the world." Jaffa can be counted on to provide a powerful defense of Lincoln, although one hardly thinks Lincoln needed a defense, but Jaffa's defense of Lincoln provides a valuable lesson on how to think and how to read. "That the seceding states had the same right of revolution as their revolutionary ancestors is of course perfectly true, for the simple reason that everyone everywhere always has this right. But it follows as well that any people anywhere has the right to suppress a revolution that they believe would endanger their rights. The people of the North had a perfect right to suppress a Southern rebellion that, in their opinion, greatly endangered the security they enjoyed under the government of the Union. . . . Mere inclination and power, taken by themselves, would indeed provide an amoral justification for such revolutions. But Lincoln calls the right of revolution a *sacred* right, which implies that it is the God-given right of the Declaration of Independence and that it may be rightly exercised only under conditions laid down in the complete doctrine of the Declaration."[42]

Paragraph twenty-nine is considered separately. It is short, consisting of three sentences. "The Chief Magistrate," Lincoln says, "derives all his authority from the people." And the people have conferred on him the power "to fix terms for the separation of the States." The people could do this themselves, "if they choose; but the executive, as such, has nothing to do with it." Jaffa in his comments, referring to his previous analysis of *Federalist* 43, states that the "law of nature is identical with sanction for the right of revolution. Hence," he reasserts "the Constitution, no less than our nation's independence, rests squarely upon the right of revolution."[43] Lincoln had said earlier in the speech that no "plainly written" right had been violated, nor had any rights of minorities been violated. Thus, as Jaffa correctly remarks, "there had been no law higher than that upon which Lincoln's government rested to justify altering or abolishing that government." Lincoln, thus claims to derive his authority from the people's original right to revolution! Jaffa comments that "[t]hroughout the war, Lincoln will take the greatest pains to prove in every instance that the authority he exercises, however extraordinary it may appear, is genuinely derived from the people by means of the Constitution and that he has exercised no authority originating in any will or purpose of his own."[44]

In paragraph thirty, Lincoln asks "Why should there not be a patient confidence in the ultimate justice of the people?" We are reminded here of the old saying, "*Vox populi, Vox Dei.*" "If the Almighty Ruler of nations, with his eternal truth and justice, be on your side of the North, or on yours of the South, that truth, and that justice, will surely prevail, by the judgment of this great tribunal, the American people." The American people will judge; they are to judge; wait for their verdict! Jaffa is right to predict that "we begin to hear the great themes of the second [inaugural]. The American people is a religious people, whose every thought and action presuppose a God who rules the world." Lincoln knew that his words would not penetrate the pride and passions of the slaveocracy, but he wanted to ensure that no path to peace was unexplored.

Jaffa comments on paragraphs thirty-one and thirty-two together. Both address the wisdom of the people embodied in the Constitution. The Executive can be voted out of office "at very short intervals" and "while the people retain their virtue and vigilance, no administration" can seriously injure the people by "extreme wickedness and folly" in the short space of four years.

Paragraph thirty-three is the theoretical center of the First Inaugural in the sense that it provoked Jaffa's deepest reflections on the theological-political question. Lincoln begins with "My countrymen . . . one and all" rather than "Fellow citizens. . ." Citizenship was in question. Once again, Lincoln counsels caution: "think calmly and *well*, upon the whole subject." Haste is the enemy of deliberation; nothing "valuable can be lost by taking time." The old Constitution, which is of your making, is unimpaired, and the current administration has no immediate power or inclination to change it. Lincoln concludes: "Christianity, and a firm reliance on Him, who has never yet forsaken this favored land, are still competent to adjust, in the best way, all our present difficulty."

Jaffa reminds us that "precipitate action has already transpired. The process of secession began almost from the moment of Lincoln's election. And secession meant abandoning the deliberative processes of the Constitution, despite the secessionists' claim to be defending the Constitution by abandoning it." The seceded states, Jaffa points out "are still at liberty to participate" in the Constitutional processes; "all they need to confirm their security under the Constitution is merely to resume their seats in the Senate."[45]

Jaffa quotes the last line of paragraph thirty-three and remarks that:

> This is one of the very few times that Lincoln, who often and with unrivaled felicity invokes the Scripture, mentions Christianity directly. Although he speaks once or twice of 'the Savior,' he never (so far as we know) pronounces the name of Jesus Christ. And he never himself professed the Christian (or any other) religion. It is undoubtedly true that Lincoln has become the greatest interpreter of America's religious destiny in part because of his distance from any sectarian religious identification. Every church or synagogue can think of him as one of their own, because he scarcely ever spoke a word inconsistent with such an assumption. By belonging to none, he belonged to all. For these reasons his mention of Christianity here is particularly arresting.[46]

Jaffa uses these observations to begin a discussion of religious freedom. "By the grace of religious freedom," Jaffa asserts, "the theological differences of Americans are not a cause of political alienation. Religious freedom under the Constitution, which blesses each church separately allows all to come together in support of that Constitution. Lincoln knows that the churches themselves had begun to divide along sectional lines. But he hopes that Christian fellowship will yet work towards reconciliation."[47] Christian fellowship might transcend political differences as all Christians, regardless of political allegiance, have more in common with one another than they do with others who have may have different political allegiances. Christians, in this regard are apolitical, their allegiance is to the kingdom of God. But within Christianity sectarian differences developed that eventually led to sectarian warfare, and we know that the wars of religion that devastated Europe were more than a distant memory to the founders. Jaffa claims that "Lincoln knew that the defenders of slavery had found in 'the curse of Canaan' a biblical defense for their position."[48] The theme that the Civil War was viewed by Jaffa as a war of religion will be examined in a later chapter.

Jaffa quoted at length from a speech that Lincoln gave in Illinois in August 1858 which "invoked the Declaration in a context that implied a perfectly nonsectarian Christianity." In that speech, the doctrine of the Founders, as embodied in the Declaration, Lincoln said, was their majestic interpretation of the economy of the Universe" which evidenced

> their lofty, wise, and noble understanding of the justice of the Creator to His creatures. . . In their enlightened belief, nothing stamped with the Divine image and likeness was sent into the world to be trodden on, and degraded, and imbruted by its fellows. They grasped not only the whole race of man then living, but they reached forward and seized upon the farthest posterity. They erected a beacon to guide their children and their children's children, and the countless myriads who should inhabit the earth in other ages. . . . so that truth, and justice, and mercy, and all the humane and Christian

> virtues might not be extinguished from the land; so that
> no man would hereafter dare to limit and circumscribe
> the great principles on which the temple of liberty was
> being built.[49]

Jaffa comments on this revelatory passage that "[t]he Founding Fathers here are apostles of the justice of the Creator to his creatures, no less than those of the Gospels. Just as the doctrine of the Declaration flows from the Golden Rule ('As I would not be a slave, so I would not be a master')[50], so is the Golden Rule implied in the Declaration. . . .The 'humane and Christian virtues' not only correspond to each other, they are the same."[51] All of this, Jaffa concludes, "is one of the great anticipations of the Gettysburg Address. The 'new birth of freedom' will reaffirm not only the principles of the Declaration of Independence but also the moral essence of the Gospels. It is in this sense that Lincoln speaks of Christianity in his inaugural." In other words, Lincoln speaks to the theological-political question which, unlike the concatenation of providential events that favored the founding, seems fated to be answered by a different providence.

In paragraph thirty-four Lincoln says, "the momentous issue of civil war" is "[i]n *your* hands, my dissatisfied fellow countrymen, and not in *mine*." There will be no conflict unless you are the aggressors. "*You* have no oath, registered in Heaven, to destroy the government, while *I* shall have the most solemn one to 'preserve, protect, and defend' it." As Jaffa rightly notes, Lincoln does not speak of secession, because secession is not "constitutionally possible." Lincoln calls the slaveocracy "my dissatisfied fellow countrymen" and not "fellow citizens" because they have become citizens—or so they supposed—of another country, one which Lincoln refused to recognize. Jaffa is right to point out that if the slaveocracy had refrained from attacking Fort Sumter and had actually supplied them and allowed the Union troops to remain "as friendly guests" it would have been impossible for Lincoln eventually to refuse to acquiesce to a peaceful separation of the Confederate states. But carried away in the throes of proslavery passion such calculations were beyond the slaveocracy, as Lincoln undoubtedly understood they would be.

Paragraph thirty-five concludes the First Inaugural when Lincoln proclaims, "I am loath to close." Jaffa says, "it seems almost impious to add commentary to such a peroration." Piety is what Lincoln seeks to awaken. Was it impious (or almost so) of Jaffa then to point out that Lincoln failed—that when he stopped talking the war came?

Chapter Three

A REEXAMINATION OF *THE HOUSE DIVIDED* IN LIGHT OF LATER DEVELOPMENTS

"The American Revolution and the American Civil War were not merely discrete events. The one led directly to the other. They constitute the first and the last acts of a single drama. The fourscore and seven years between the Declaration of Independence and the Gettysburg Address comprehend that action of a tremendous world-historical tragedy."

—HARRY JAFFA—
How to Think About the American Revolution

Harry Jaffa writes in *Crisis of the House Divided* that "Lincoln . . . is supposed to have written the Gettysburg Address on the back of an envelope as he rode from Washington. Yet a careful reading of [an] earlier deliverance will show that the ideas crystalized in 1863, in prose not unworthy of the greatest master of our language, had been pondered and matured full twenty-five years before." Jaffa, of course, is referring to Lincoln's "Address Before the Young Men's Lyceum of Springfield, Illinois," delivered on January 27, 1838. Lincoln gave two early complimentary speeches, the Lyceum address, addressing politics, and the "Temperance Address," in 1842 dealing with morality. The theme of the two speeches is how a nation based on the consent of the governed can be self-governing. The question of morality is a question of the passions. A self-governing people must, first of all, be capable of governing themselves as individuals, and that means controlling their passions. It is a matter of habituation to obeying good passions and avoiding bad passions. Once an individual becomes capable of governing himself, he can join with fellow citizens in a self-governing nation that derives its just powers from the consent of the governed. Consent in a self-governing nation must be informed or reasonable, which is to say that the constitution of a self-governing nation must facilitate majority rule, at the same time that it guarantees minority rights; the majority must rule in a manner that recognizes the limits placed on its rule by the requirements of the "Laws of Nature and Nature's God." In other words, the majority must be capable of ruling itself. Ruling and being ruled in turn is the electoral mode that is demanded by a republican form of government, and it is self-governance that forms that basis for republican virtues. As Jaffa puts it, "[f]or men claiming republican freedom—the right to self-government, a right whose very name is a synonym for virtue—cannot doubt that they must vindicate their claim by virtue."[1]

Lincoln, Emancipation, and Political Religion

In *Crisis of the House Divided*, Jaffa argued that once it became possible for Lincoln to foresee the end of slavery, he prepared himself for a role in emancipation, and even, in the Lyceum speech, gave a "prophetic account of the coming crisis" casting himself in the role of Emancipator! Lincoln warned of future dangers that would confront the nation. These would be internal dangers, principally those stemming from mob rule, or more precisely the "spirit of mob rule." The lawless in spirit—those who tolerate lawlessness—will be prone to become "lawless in fact." Lincoln, of course, without direct acknowledgement, referred to abolitionists, who advocated violating the Constitution in order to emancipate slaves, whereas Lincoln's avowed policy was one of prudence, which was to observe strict adherence to the Constitution which, when understood in light of the principles of the Declaration, had put slavery on the course of "ultimate extinction." The greatest danger engendered by the "mobocratic spirit," Lincoln insisted, "which all must admit, is now abroad in the land, [is that] the strongest bulwark of any Government, and particularly of those constituted like ours, may effectually be broken down and destroyed—I mean the *attachment* of the People."[2] What can unite them? What is the remedy Lincoln proposes? A political religion!

Let every American swear, Lincoln pleads,

> by the blood of the Revolution never to violate the Constitution and the laws of the country or tolerate their violation by others. As the patriots of seventy-six did to the support of the Declaration of Independence, so to the support of the Constitution and Laws, let every American pledge his life, his property, and sacred honor;—let every man remember that to violate the law, is to trample on the blood of his father, and to tear the charter of his own, and his children's liberty. Let reverence for the laws, be breathed by every American mother, to the lisping babe, that prattles in her lap—let it be taught

in schools, in seminaries, and in colleges;—. . . and in short, let it become the *political religion* of the nation; and let the old and the young, the rich and the poor, the grave and the gay, of all sexes and tongues, and colors and conditions, sacrifice unceasingly upon its altars.[3]

Will this remedy be sufficient to insulate the nation against those ambitious men who would not be satisfied with "a seat in Congress," or "a presidential chair," those men of all-consuming ambition, who belong to the "family of the lion, or the tribe of the eagle," those destroyers of republics such as "an Alexander, a Caesar, or a Napoleon." The men of great ambition will not be satisfied to follow the paths of others but will seek new paths of their own making, because as Lincoln notes in his best poetic imagery:

Towering genius disdains a beaten path. It seeks regions hitherto unexplored. It sees *no distinction* in adding story to story upon the monuments of fame, erected to the memory of others. It *denies* that it is glory enough to serve under any chief. It *scorns* to tread in the footsteps of *any* predecessor, however illustrious. It thirsts and burns; and, if possible, it will have it, whether at the expense of emancipating slaves, or enslaving freemen. Is it unreasonable then to expect, that some man possessed of the loftiest genius, coupled with ambition sufficient to push it to the utmost stretch, will at some time, spring up among us? And when such a one does, it will require the people to be united with each other, attached to the government and laws, and generally intelligent to successfully frustrate his designs.[4]

Lincoln's "political religion" is essentially a question of

political opinion. We saw in the previous chapter some of Lincoln's attempts to expose the contradictions of Douglas's campaign. But the volatility of public opinion—goaded on by Douglas's "don't care" policy—challenged Lincoln's republican statesmanship and his defense of founding principles. Surely the political religion described by Lincoln, in his best imitation of a sermon from an elevated pulpit, would be ineffective against an Alexander, Caesar, or Napoleon, all of whom knew how to appeal to the sentiments of republican citizens. Indeed, it would take one of their kind—someone of great ambition—but someone who was willing to save a republic, not destroy it, to gratify his ambitions. Does such a man exist? Is human nature capable of yielding such magnanimity? Lincoln demonstrated that he was well-aware that ambition was neutral; that it could be served by freeing slaves or enslaving freemen. The man of superior ambition however—a godlike man among men—would be willing only to gratify his ambitions by serving just ends, by enlarging freedom for all, never contracting it for anyone, including those currently held in slavery.

Can the Magnanimous Man Save a Republic (Or Even Live in a Republic)?

"At this point," Jaffa argues, the Lyceum Speech takes "an unexpected turn. . . . We find the future author of the Gettysburg Address denying, in a wholly relevant sense, that all men are equal." The "famous proposition" that "all men are created equal," "[a]lthough it has given rise to countless differing interpretations," no longer "indisputably" means that "the government of man by man, unlike the government

of beasts by man" is "founded in any natural difference between rulers and ruled?"[5] After pointing out that Lincoln in
the Gettysburg Address called the "phrase 'all men are created equal' a *'proposition,'* Jaffa explains that in the Lyceum
Address Lincoln "tells us that there are men whose genius
for and will to domination virtually makes them a species
apart." "Even as it is natural and rational for men who are
equal to seek in consent the basis of political rule, so is it natural (and rational) for men who are surpassingly superior to
seek in the unfettered acknowledgment of their superiority
the basis of such rule." They are the enemies of any political
regime that they do not rule; this is especially true, of course,
of republics.

Jaffa discusses Aristotle's view of the "god-like" men who
arise in political communities who are so superior in talents
and abilities and for whom the rule of law would be unjust
because they are themselves a law unto themselves. This is
not unlike the passage in Matthew that was discussed in a
previous chapter when it was reported that when the 'ἔθνη
or pagans, "who have not the law [of Moses] do by nature
(φύσει) what the law [of Moses] requires, they are a law unto
themselves." Those who are so superior by nature would
therefore be treated unjustly if made to follow the law. Aristotle said that democracies typically would ostracize such
individuals for specified periods or permanently to avoid the
injustice of having someone who is a law unto himself be
subject to the law. The superiority of such individuals is a
clear and present danger to democracies, whether they submit to the law or seek recognition of their superiority. The
biblical injunction, I say, conveys the same message.

Lincoln makes no suggestion of ostracism, because a
regime based on consent, means the consent of all, and

ambition, absent an overt act amounting to treason would almost certainly preclude ostracism and even then the issue of cruel and unusual punishment would arise.

Lincoln's conception of the "nature of true statesman in the highest sense," Jaffa argues, is the one "who can forgo the honors of his countrymen."[6] Describing Aristotle's great-souled man, Jaffa avers, that "he alone is worthy of the highest honor who holds honor itself in contempt, who prefers even to the voice of his countrymen the approving voice heard only by himself. 'Well done, thou good and faithful servant.'"[7] This last quote is from the Parable of the Talents in Matthew 25:14, where the master, before leaving for a long absence, entrusts property (τούς ᾽ιδίους) to three servants (δούλους), giving 5 talents to one, 2 to another, and 1 to the last. The talents are thus proportioned 5-2-1, to each according to his ability. Upon his return the master found that the servant entrusted with 5 talents had traded and doubled his money; the second, having received 2 talents did the same; but the third, buried his 1 talent in the ground for safekeeping, saying that I knew you to be a hard master, reaping where you did not sow, and gathering where you did not plant. I was afraid and returned your mina. Those who doubled the investment received the praise quoted in part by Jaffa: "Well done, good and faithful servant; you have been faithful over a little, I will set you over much; enter into the joy of your master." The third servant who acted out of fear and did not increase the property, was scorned by the master: "You wicked and slothful servant! You knew that I reap where I have not sowed, and gather where I have not planted? Then you ought to have invested my money with the bankers, and at my coming I should have received what was my own with interest." There is, of course, much debate about the interpretation of this biblical passage, but there is little doubt about Jaffa's use of it. Charles Kesler points out that "to be a 'good and faithful servant' is not quite the same thing as the magnanimous man's pride and pleasure in knowing that, compared to himself, 'nothing is great.' Strictly speaking, the magnanimous man does not conceive of himself as a servant to anyone or anything not even virtue, which for him is inseparable from the actions and contemplation of his own; like the gods, he is a benefactor, not a servant." In using the biblical quotation, Kesler continues, Jaffa puts together the classical political philosophy of Aristotle and Christianity, thus suggesting that "Lincoln's understanding of himself transcended that of a magnanimous man. Whether this transcendence was in the direction of the love of God or the love of the Good or both is a difficult question, which Jaffa did not explicitly answer." Kesler suggests an answer, however, that was almost certainly Jaffa's answer: "Certainly, the Biblical God is a god of particular providence and of moral actions, and so is a source of duties and a kind of model for statesmanship as well as salvation."[8] This, of course, is what Jaffa means when he called Lincoln "the prophetic statesman of a people, like Israel of old."[9]

Can Nations Be Magnanimous?

In what must be considered an extraordinary extension of the argument, Jaffa also contends that nations can be magnanimous. "The Lyceum speech," Jaffa wrote, "recorded the discovery in the soul of 'towering genius' that the highest ambition can be conceived as consummated only in the highest service, that egotism and altruism ultimately coincide in that consciousness of superiority which is superiority in the ability to benefit others." The same "towering genius" can characterize the people of a "superior nation." Thus, Jaffa asserts:

> Lincoln argues in the course of his debates with Douglas that the freedom of a free people resides above all in that consciousness of freedom which is also a consciousness of self-imposed restraints. The heart of Lincoln's case for popular government is the vindication of the people's cause on the highest grounds which had hitherto been claimed for aristocratic forms. In the consciousness of a strength which is not abused is a consciousness of a greater strength, and therewith a greater pride and a greater pleasure, than can be known by those who do not know how to deny themselves.[10]

Strictly parsed, this means, I say, that Lincoln viewed the American regime as a true aristocracy operating in the only way a "true aristocracy" could—in the *form* of a democracy in which there were no pre-ordained class or caste barriers to the advancement of the natural talents and abilities of those who would emerge as the *natural aristoi*. Near the beginning of *Liberalism Ancient and Modern*, in the first essay, "What is Liberal Education," Leo Strauss opines that democracy "is meant to be an aristocracy which has broadened into a universal aristocracy. Prior to the emergence of modern democracy some doubts were felt whether democracy thus understood is possible. As one of the two greatest minds among the theorists of democracy put it, 'If there were a people consisting of gods, it would rule itself democratically. A government of such perfection is not suitable for human beings.'" Strauss does not name the second greatest mind on democracy, but every reader would recognize the quotation from

Rousseau's *Social Contract*. Whether Strauss is casting doubt on "democracy thus understood" by citing Rousseau, or indulging some obvious irony is a question.[11] But we must also remember his statement in a later essay in the same book, "Liberal Education and Responsibility," where he says "that wisdom requires unhesitating loyalty to a decent constitution and even to the cause of constitutionalism."[12] Perhaps the most important statement made by Strauss was in his "Restatement on Xenophon's *Hiero*," which was a reply to Alexandre Kojeve, Strauss's long-time friend and Hegelian. (It was only learned after Strauss had died that his old friend had been a Stalinist and unapologetic apparatchik of the Soviet Union.) Strauss wrote that "[i]t would not be difficult to show that the classical argument cannot be disposed of as easily as is now generally thought, and that liberal or constitutional democracy comes closer to what the classics demanded than any alternative that is viable in our age."[13]

We also cannot forget Strauss's citation, in his own name, of Jefferson, that the best form of government is the one which "provides the most effectually for a pure selection of [the] natural *aristoi* into the offices of government." In the sentence preceding the one quoted by Strauss, Jefferson had argued that nature or creation would have been "inconsistent . . . to have formed man for the social state, and not to have provided virtue and wisdom enough to manage the concerns of the society." The existence of the natural *aristoi* is thus proof for Jefferson that "creation" has designed man for the social or political state! Man is by nature a political animal, and the best regime by nature is aristocracy. And since it is evident that "virtue and talent" have been "by nature . . . scattered with equal hand through all its conditions," a system of equal opportunity allowing virtue and talent to rise from all classes would be most consistent with "natural right."[14] Scarcity in the ancient world prevented the actualization of the best regime by nature; "emancipation of acquisitiveness" was the necessary precondition for a regime that could adopt equal opportunity as its principle of distributive justice. Thus, the best regime of classical political philosophy became realizable only on the grounds of a radically transformed notion of the right to property and a scheme of constitutional government designed to protect the right to property. Even though the right to private property is wholly modern—and the "emancipation of acquisition" *wholly alien* to classical political philosophy—it is impossible not to see, as I am convinced Strauss did—the influence of Aristotelian natural right at work in the American founding, which, for the first time, held out the prospect that genuine aristocracy based on natural talents and abilities could replace the pseudo-aristocracies of birth and class that had dominated the past. Equality of opportunity—not the accident of birth—was to be the principle of distributive justice that would animate the American regime.

The following extended quotation from Strauss, from his essay "Liberal Education and Responsibility," in *Liberalism Ancient and Modern*, could have been written by Jefferson. From the discussion we have just unfolded, it is beyond cavil that it is written in the spirit of Jefferson. Let us read it in that spirit. Strauss, painting in rather broad—but revealing—strokes, says that:

> It is a demand of justice that there should be a reasonable correspondence between the social hierarchy and the natural hierarchy. The lack of such a correspondence in the old scheme was defended by the fundamental fact of scarcity. With the increasing abundance it became

increasingly possible to see and to admit the element of hypocrisy which had entered into the traditional notion of aristocracy; the existing aristocracies were proved to be oligarchies, rather than aristocracies. In other words it became increasingly easy to argue from the premise that natural inequality has very little to do with social inequality, that practically or politically speaking one may safely assume that all are by nature equal, that all men have the same natural rights, provided one uses this rule of thumb as the major premise for reaching the conclusion that everyone should be given the same opportunity as everyone else; natural inequality has its rightful place in the use, nonuse, or abuse of opportunity in the race as distinguished from at the start. Thus it became possible to abolish many injustices or at least many things which had become injustices."[15]

Strauss never mentions America, but there can be little doubt that he is referring to the American constitutional system, especially when considered in light of the remark that we have already quoted that "wisdom requires unhesitating loyalty to a decent constitution and even to the cause of constitutionalism." Distributive justice and equality as discussed in this quotation is easily traced to an important Platonic source that was the subject of Strauss's last book—Plato's *Laws*. It is, of course, always dangerous to quote the words of a speaker in a dialogue because it abstracts from the drama or action of the dialogue.[16] With that warning, I will quote from the Athenian Stranger who is the philosopher-founder a new city, not in speech, but in deed: "distributive justice" in this new city will be made "according to nature" [viz., natural talents]. This is called by the philosopher "the truest and best equality"—"the natural equality given on each occasion to unequal men."[17] Here, the Athenian Stranger, Thomas Jefferson, and Leo Strauss meet on common ground.[18]

Lincoln's Eulogy of Henry Clay

On July 6, 1852, Lincoln gave his "Eulogy on Henry Clay." He began in a seemingly unusual way by quoting the eulogy of a Democratic Party newspaper. Professor Michael Zuckert reports that the quotation from the earlier eulogy takes up one-fifth of Lincoln's own eulogy. Zuckert defends the lengthy quotation, arguing that "[t]he sincerity and truth of praise by a political opponent are more trustworthy than the biased and self-interested praise of a political ally. Besides, Lincoln tells us, he 'could not, in any language of [his] own so well express [his] thought.' These are good reasons, certainly," Zuckert concludes, without pausing to consider whether these last remarks of Lincoln might be highly ironic.[19] In the highly suspicious passage in question, the eulogy of the Democratic Party newspaper had printed this:

> Perchance, in the whole circle of the great and gifted of our land, there remains but one on whose shoulders the mighty mantle of the departed statesman may fall—one, while we now write, is doubtless pouring his tears over the bier of his brother and his friend—brother, friend ever, yet in political sentiment, as far apart as party could make them. Ah, it is at times like these, that the petty distinctions of mere party disappear. We see only the great, the grand, the noble features of the departed statesman. . ."

Professor Zuckert rightly points out that the unidentified person "upon whose shoulders the mighty mantle of the departed statesman may fall" is Stephen A. Douglas, who was instrumental in passing through Congress the settlement that had been negotiated by Henry Clay.[20] The effective credit for avoiding a slavery crisis, according to this "non-partisan account" belongs to Douglas, not Clay. At the same time, everything that follows Lincoln's quotation of the Democratic Party newspaper must be considered as a dialectical refutation of its argument—and by extension of Stephen Douglas. Lincoln's concentration on Clay's anti-slavery credentials, of course, is aimed directly at Douglas. Lincoln's Eulogy of Clay, in my opinion, should be considered as the opening salvo of what would become the Lincoln–Douglas debates!

John Channing Briggs has rightly said that the "Great Compromise of 1850, which was negotiated through Congress by Stephen Douglas, would discandy,[21] revealing deepening sectional divisions over slavery that were splitting the Whigs and threatening to break up the Democrats."[22] Briggs sees clearly Lincoln's central intention in the Clay eulogy: "Lincoln was preparing himself, his fellow Whigs, and his general audience for a new political alignment. . . ." Lincoln's ambitions, however, reached further than a new political realignment. Briggs suggests Lincoln sought a new "political philosophy." This I believe is incorrect. Lincoln's political philosophy was fully formed, but he now needed a cause worthy of his ambitions. Douglas's repeal of the Kansas-Nebraska Act, which, as we have already discussed, Lincoln considered as the equivalent of the repeal of the Declaration itself, was his call to action. His serious career as a politician and statesman began with his speech at Peoria in 1854, and the Peoria speech was a fully developed account of his political philosophy.

Less than a year after the speech at Peoria on October 16, 1854, Lincoln wrote a letter to George Robertson, an acquaintance and law professor at Transylvania University in Kentucky, and author of a collection of speeches and articles on law he had endorsed for Lincoln. Lincoln wrote to thank him for the copy he had left in his absence. In one of your speeches, Lincoln wrote, "you spoke of '*the peaceful extinction of slavery*.'" Lincoln, however, forcefully countered, "I think that there is no peaceful extinction of slavery in prospect for us. The signal failure of Henry Clay, and other good and great men, in 1849, to effect any thing in favor of gradual emancipation in Kentucky, together with a thousand other signs, extinguishes that hope utterly." Lincoln ended the letter with language that was to be featured in the House Divided Speech three years later, a speech that ended all possibility of compromise on the issue of slavery: "Our political problem now is 'Can we, as a nation, continue together *permanently—forever*—half slave, and half free?' The problem is too mighty for me. May God, in his mercy, superintend the solution."[23] As it turns out, the "problem," although great, was not "too mighty" for Lincoln, whose prudent statesmanship, while it could not control events, was not simply the result of the uncontrollable forces of history.[24]

Before addressing the House Divided Speech, it is necessary first to take notice of a little remarked speech Lincoln made on October 30, at the end of the 1858 campaign for Senate in Illinois. No transcript of the speech survives, but Lincoln carefully prepared the conclusion of the speech, and the manuscript is printed in the *Collected Works* as "Fragment: Last Speech of the Campaign at Springfield, Illinois." The passage on "ambition" will be most interesting for an approach to the House Divided Speech. Lincoln said:

Ambition has been ascribed to me. God knows how sincerely I prayed from the first that this field of ambition might not be opened. I claim no insensibility to political honors; but today could the Missouri restriction be restored, and the whole slavery question replaced on the old ground of 'toleration' by *necessity* where it exists, with unyielding hostility to the spread of it, on principle, I would, in consideration, gladly agree, that Judge Douglas should never be *out*, and I never *in*, an office, so long we both or either, live.[25]

How this serves as a kind of post-facto introduction to the House Divided Speech will become evident in due course.

I think it is abundantly clear that the Democratic Party newspaper eulogy of Henry Clay, Professor Zuckert to the contrary notwithstanding, was a partisan appeal to Horace Greeley and his ilk who were urging the Republicans to support Douglas for president because of his "availability" and "electability." This accounts for the exaggerated praise of the "bipartisanship" of Douglas. And this was the grooming of Douglas for a presidential run in 1852! If I am right that Lincoln's eulogy was a dialectical refutation of the Democratic eulogy, then, as previously mentioned, this was the first of the Lincoln–Douglas debates!

Biblical References in the House Divided Speech

Matthew Holbreich and Danelo Petranovich correctly point out that in the House Divided speech Lincoln uses biblical imagery three times.[26] The first is one of the most quoted passages of Lincoln's: "A house divided against itself cannot stand."[27] It is, of course, the biblical passage that gives the speech its name. Lincoln continues:

> I believe this government cannot endure, permanently half *slave* and half *free*. I do not expect the Union to be *dissolved*—I do not expect the house to *fall*—but I *do* expect it will cease to be divided. It will become *all* one thing, or *all* the other. Either the *opponents* of slavery, will arrest the further spread of it, and place it where the public mind shall rest in the belief that it is in course of ultimate extinction; or its *advocates* will push it forward, till it shall become alike lawful in *all* the States, *old* as well as *new*—*North* as well as *South*.[28]

We have already seen the anticipation of this language in the letter to George Robertson three years earlier, albeit expressed in somewhat more pessimistic terms. Holbreich and Petranovich summarize the biblical accounts in this way:

> There are three sources for this citation [viz., "a house divided against itself cannot stand"], all of which tell the same story: Mark 3, Matthew 12 and Luke 11. Jesus entered the Temple where some scribes were assembled, as well as a man with a deformed hand. Jesus healed his hand. Given that this was the Sabbath, and healing (in the interpretation of the scribes) was proscribed on the Sabbath, they denounced Jesus. This story from the Gospel can be easily read as a metaphor for the American political situation. It pits healing, and thus the achievement of a concrete good, against conformity with the traditional law. It is the traditional law that impedes healing the deformed hand. Lincoln always argued that he thought the Federal Government had no power to interfere with slavery where it already existed. But

the Union cannot last half-slave and half-free. It must, therefore, be Lincoln's intent to eventually see slavery abolished where the writ of the Federal Government cannot run. The Constitution prevents the objective that Lincoln announces in the opening of his speech. But Lincoln does not think that the problem will be solved until a crisis will have been reached and passed.[29]

In the main, the authors' account of Lincoln's use of the biblical account is unobjectionable, but it is woefully incomplete and being incomplete it distorts Lincoln's purpose in choosing to emphasize the "House Divided" passage. Holbeich and Petranovich say that the scribes "denounced Jesus." The Greek however indicates that the verb that was used (ἀπολέσωσιν) meant that the scribes planned "to destroy" Jesus, and that Jesus, knowing the intention of the scribes asked his many followers not to reveal him.

But the most important part of Matthew 12 (which was certainly the account Lincoln used) was left undiscussed by Holbreich and Petranovich. A blind and dumb demoniac was brought to Jesus and Jesus healed him and he was able to speak and see. But when the Pharisees (scribes) heard they said, "it is only by Be-elzebub, the prince (ἄρχοντι = ruler) of demons, that this one (Οὗτος) casts out demons." Knowing how the Pharisees thought, Jesus said to them: "Every kingdom divided against itself is laid waste, and *no city or house divided against itself will stand*; and if Satan casts out Satan, he is divided against himself; how then will his kingdom stand." Jesus then announces that "if it is by the spirit of God that I cast out demons, then the kingdom of God has come upon you." Jesus thus argues, almost in the form of a dialectical refutation of the Pharisees Socrates would surely have admired, that the Kingdom of Satan is a House Divided Against Itself and therefore cannot stand. I am fairly confident that Lincoln recognized the dialectical character of this argument and that is why it became the theme of his decisive speech. Here, Jesus, Socrates, and Lincoln stand united.

We are reminded of the final Lincoln–Douglas debate where Lincoln made a similar dialectical refutation of Douglas's contradictory attachment to the *Dred Scott* decision. Jaffa describes the peroration of Lincoln's final speech in the debates: "Douglas might accept *Dred Scott*, and with it slave codes for the territories, or he might oppose slave codes and reject *Dred Scott*. The links in Lincoln's chain of argument were unbreakable. By exploiting as he did Douglas's refusal to reject *Dred Scott*, Lincoln burned Douglas's bridges to the Republican Party and the free soil movement. By exploiting as he did Douglas's refusal to accept the obligation under *Dred Scott* to protect the slave owner in his rights in the territories, Lincoln burned Douglas's bridges to the proslavery South in its determination to insist upon slave codes as its price to remain in the Union." In his praise of Lincoln's dialectical refutation of Douglas, Jaffa bestowed on him, the highest praise he ever awarded: "It is doubtful if Socratic rationalism ever appeared more powerfully in public utterance since the founder of political philosophy walked the streets of Athens."[30] The only reason the comparison to Matthew is inappropriate is that Jesus made his dialectical refutation in private.

A Living Dog and a Dead Lion

In the House Divided Speech, Lincoln made this unusual biblical allusion: "They remind us that *he* [viz. Douglas] is a very *great man* and that the largest of *us* are very small ones. Let this be granted. But 'a living dog is better than a *dead lion*,' Judge Douglas, if not a *dead* lion for *this work*, is at least a *caged* and *toothless* one. How can he oppose the advances of slavery? He don't *care* any thing about it. His avowed *mission is impressing* the 'public heart' to *care* nothing about it."[31] Holbreich and Petranovich rightly note that Lincoln's comparison of himself to a living dog and Douglas to a dead lion doesn't advance Lincoln's argument or contribute to his rhetorical strategy.[32] Why does he use this image that he obviously knew was from *Ecclesiastes*?[33] The passage in context, I believe, becomes clear. The "Philosopher" who narrates the passages of *Ecclesiastes* states ten lines later that:

> There was a little city, and few men within it; and there came a great king against it, and besieged it, and built great bulwarks against it. Now there was found in it a poor wise man, and he by his wisdom delivered the city; yet no man remembered that same poor man. Then said I, Wisdom is better than strength: nevertheless the poor man's wisdom is despised and his words are not heard.[34]

Matthew Holbreich and Danilo Petranovich argue that this passage from Ecclesiastes "fits quite well with Lincoln's public image. He is the poor man from the woods, who had a high opinion of his own wisdom, had a great ambition, and an idea that he would save his country, but also a deep melancholic worry that he would eventually be forgotten."[35] We have already seen Jaffa's argument that Lincoln's ambitions were magnanimous and utterly indifferent to recognition or approval and hardly driven by "melancholic worry." The passage from Ecclesiastes is a description of a magnanimous man who is indifferent to the recognition of his fellow citizens for

Chapter Three

the great deeds he has performed and finds it sufficient that his ambitions are gratified by the self-recognition that he has that his deeds were intrinsically just and thereby beneficial. Lincoln certainly knew that his reference to living dogs and dead lions would lead worthy inquirers to these passages.

We Gathered from the Four Winds

Near the end of the House Divided speech is a biblical reference that is difficult to detect. Lincoln describes the emergence of the Republican Party:

> Two years ago the Republicans of the nation mustered over thirteen hundred thousand strong.
>
> We did this under the single impulse of resistance to a common danger, with every external circumstance against us.
>
> Of strange, discordant, and even, hostile elements, we gathered from the four winds, and formed and fought the battle through, under the constant hot fire of a disciplined, proud, and pampered enemy.
>
> Did we brave all then to falter now?—now—when that same enemy is wavering, dissevered and belligerent?
>
> The result is not doubtful. We shall not fail—if we stand firm, we shall not fail.[36]

"We gathered from the four winds" evokes the language of Ezekiel: "The Lord God said to me, 'Prophesy to these bones, and say to them, O dry bones, hear the word of the LORD. Thus says the LORD GOD to these bones: Behold, I will cause breath to enter you, and you shall live. And I will lay sinews upon you, and will cause flesh to come upon you, and

117

cover you with skin, and put breath in you, and you shall live; and you shall know that I am the LORD." And Ezekiel sees that "there were sinews on them, and flesh had come upon them, and skin had covered them; but there was no breath in them." Then the Lord said to Ezekiel, "prophesy, son of man and say to the breath. Thus says the LORD GOD: come from the four winds, O breath, and breathe upon these slain, that they may live." And Ezekiel reports, so they did, and became "an exceedingly great host."[37]

Matthew Holbreich and Danilo Petranovich comment that "[l]ike the smiting of Egypt because of its sins, Ezekiel prophesied and then later heard of the fall of Egypt because of its sins and idol worship. After the loss of Jerusalem he prophesized the restoration and rebirth of the Hebrew nation." The authors point out that that the Ezekiel theme occurs not only in the Temperance address, but also in in the eulogy of Henry Clay, where Lincoln rehearses the theme that Egypt is punished "as a slave holding nation."[38] Holbreich and Petranovich argue that Lincoln compares "the Americans to the slave-holding Egyptians. It is the Americans who shall be judged by God and incur his divine wrath for their sins if they do not purify themselves and complete their revolution."[39] The result of all this is that the Republican Party, since the election of 1852, has become a great host, a great army, for the unity of America just as "Ezekiel prophesied . . . the restoration and rebirth of the Hebrew nation" as a single, unified nation. "Lincoln's Biblical citation clearly reveals his purpose: to unify the nation, purified of the sin of slavery, under the banner of freedom." "Lincoln's intentions were not so deeply veiled," the authors continue, "nor his allusions so obscure that his critics did not perceive his true positions. Right after the House Divided speech he was in fact accused of wanting to destroy slavery in the South."[40] As proof, Holbreich and Petranovich cite the famous letter Lincoln wrote to John L. Scripps, editor of the *Chicago Daily Democrat*, a week after the House Divided speech, answering Scripps's enquiry as to what Lincoln meant when he said that slavery must be placed "where the public mind shall rest in the belief that it is in course of ultimate extinction." Lincoln wrote that "I have declared a thousand times, and now repeat that, in my opinion, neither the General Government, nor any other power outside of the slave states, can constitutionally or rightfully interfere with slaves or slavery where it already exists. I believe that whenever the effort to spread slavery into the new territories by whatever means, and into the free states themselves, by Supreme court decisions, shall be fairly headed off, the institution will then be in course of ultimate extinction; and by the language used I meant only this."[41] The two authors use the Scripps letter as an example of Lincoln's political acumen—and so it is. "As a senatorial candidate, he was too savvy to commit political suicide. But Lincoln's constant return to Ezekiel, especially in a speech as significant and provocative as this one, reveals the structure of Lincoln's moral and political imagination. Lincoln envisioned the eradication of slavery in terms of a moral resurrection."[42] There can be no doubt, I say, about the authors' conclusion about "a moral resurrection."

Jaffa's Forensic Defense of the House Divided Speech

Harry Jaffa, however, adumbrates a better forensic defense of Lincoln's argument in the House Divided speech that there was a "tendency" for the national legalization of slavery. "[I]t is important to keep in mind," Jaffa writes,

> that the evidence Lincoln assembles in the speech is not
> so much evidence of a plot as it is evidence of a tenden-
> cy toward a condition in which slavery shall be lawful
> everywhere in the United States. Lincoln was careful
> then and thereafter to point out that he did not know
> a conspiracy existed, only that he believed it. All his ev-
> idence, so far as a plot is concerned, is circumstantial.
> Yet the vital question which we must ask is not whether
> the circumstances overwhelmingly suggest pre-concert
> among the principals concerned in them but wheth-
> er they overwhelmingly indicate a tendency toward
> spreading slavery.[43]

Do subsequent events support Lincoln's predictions? Jaffa's
answer is an unequivocal "yes."[44] Lincoln in the House Divided speech rehearses the activities of the four "workmen,"
Stephen Douglas, Franklin Pierce, Roger Taney and James
Buchanan, admitting, "we can not absolutely *know*" that the

> exact adaptations are the result of preconcert. But when
> we see a lot of framed timbers, different portions of
> which we know have been gotten out at different times
> and places and by different workmen. . . and when we
> see these timbers joined together, and see they exactly
> make the frame of a house or a mill, all the tenons and
> mortices exactly fitting, and all the lengths and propor-
> tions of the different pieces exactly adapted to their re-
> spective places, and not a piece too many or too few—
> not omitting even scaffolding—or, if a single piece be
> lacking, we can see the place in the frame exactly fitted
> and prepared to yet bring such piece in—in *such* a case,
> we find it impossible to not *believe* that Stephen and

> Franklin and Roger and James all understood one another from the beginning, and all worked upon a common *plan* or *draft* drawn up before the first lick was struck.[45]

The piece that was missing, but for which a place was carefully prepared, was, of course, the *Dred Scott* decision. How did the pre-concert or conspiracy proceed in this matter? Stephen Douglas, the author of the Kansas-Nebraska Act had repeatedly stated on the floor of the Senate that the constitutionality of the act was a matter to be determined by the Supreme Court.[46] President Franklin Pierce in his message to Congress in December, 1855 had mused that the Missouri Compromise "restrictions were, in the estimation of many thoughtful men, null from the beginning, unauthorized by the Constitution . . . and inconsistent with the equality of these States." And in his last message to Congress in December, 1856, delivered while the *Dred Scott* decision was under deliberation by the Supreme Court, Pierce pronounced the Missouri Compromise law a "mere nullity" and a "monument of error and a beacon of warning to the legislature and the statesman."[47] At his inaugural on March 4, 1857, before he gave his inaugural speech president-elect Buchanan exchanged some words with Chief Justice Taney that were inaudible to onlookers. In his inaugural speech, Buchanan make these remarkable—not to say shocking—remarks: The question of slavery in the territories is "a judicial question which legitimately belongs to the Supreme Court of the United States, before whom it is now pending, and will, it is understood, be speedily and finally settled. To their decision, in common with all good citizens, I shall cheerfully submit, whatever this may be, though it has ever been my individual opinion that, under the Kansas–Nebraska Act, the appropriate period will be when the number of actual residents in the Territory shall justify the formation of a Constitution with a view to its admission as a state."[48] Almost immediately after the speech it was revealed that the newly inaugurated president had been in correspondence with two members of the Supreme Court, Justices Catron and Grier, the latter of whom wrote in a letter to Buchanan, a week before his inauguration, that in the impending *Dred Scott* decision there would be "six, if not seven . . . who will decide the Compromise law of 1820 to be of *non-effect*."[49] Grier's prediction was correct; the final result was 7–2, with dissents from Justices Curtis and McClean. Near the conclusion of his majority opinion, Chief Justice Taney wrote that "the right of property in a slave is distinctly and expressly affirmed in the Constitution."[50] Since the Constitution is the supreme law of the land under Article VI of the Constitution, states are bound by rulings of the United States Supreme Court. Was it too much of a stretch for Lincoln to predict a "second *Dred Scott*" case in which states would be precluded from preventing slavery in the same way that territories had been in *Dred Scott*? But as Lincoln vigorously and often pointed out, the Constitution did not "distinctly and expressly" affirm "the right of property in a slave" for the simple reason that "slave" or "slavery" never appears in the Constitution, and whenever there is any allusion to that "peculiar institution," the circumlocutions of "person" or "persons held to service" is used. Strictly speaking, under the Fifth Amendment no "person" can be "deprived of life, liberty, or property, without due process of law." The question that was debated throughout the 1850s was simply whether a slave was a person or property. Lincoln, of course, took his stand on the principle of the Declaration that "all men are created equal." For Lincoln, there was no question that the founders included blacks of African descent, as well as every member of the human species in this all-inclusive phrase. Taney, on the other hand, simply stated that the founders regarded blacks of African descent as articles of commerce to be bought and sold whenever a profit could be made. They were not part of the people, whether slave or free, who "framed and adopted" the Constitution.[51] Justice Benjamin Curtis, in dissent, however, pointed out a factual error in Taney's opinion. In five states, free blacks were allowed to vote in the ratification election for the Constitution and he acknowledges there is evidence that they did so.[52] Blacks of African descent *were* in fact part of the people who *ratified* the Constitution, thus making them part of the people of the United States.

When Lincoln examined the *Dred Scott* case, he must have been alarmed to read the last paragraph of Justice Nelson's concurring opinion which seemed to foretell his prediction of a "second *Dred Scott*" decision. One competent scholar has written that Nelson's opinion was written as if he had in mind the New York case of *Lemmon v. The People* (1860).[53] "A question has been alluded to," Nelson wrote, "on the argument, namely:

> the right of the master with his slave of transit into or through a free State, on business or commercial pursuits, or in the exercise of a federal right, or the discharge of a federal duty, being a citizen of the United States, which is not before us. This question depends upon different considerations and principles from the one in hand, and turns upon the rights and privileges secured to a common citizen of the republic under the Constitution of the United States. When that question arises, we shall be prepared to decide it.[54]

In the concurring opinion that followed immediately upon Nelson's opinion, Justice Grier wrote, "I concur in the opinion delivered by Mr. Justice Nelson on the questions discussed by him," without saying specifically what he would be willing to rule on the question of slavery in free states. But I believe the implication was clear enough.

Lincoln certainly knew about the case of *Lemmon v. The People* decided by the New York Court of Appeals in March 1860 since reference was made to it in the printed version of his Cooper Union speech. Although the speech was delivered before the decision was handed down, a note in the pamphlet reproducing the speech—a publication that Lincoln supervised—referred to the case.[55] The New York Court of Appeals had held that a slave brought from Virginia to the port of New York to be transshipped to another slave-holding state refused to honor an Article IV privileges and immunities claim by the owner, holding that his status as a citizen of another State did not give him the right to a privilege and immunity that a citizen of New York was not entitled to: "[A] citizen of this State cannot bring a slave within its limits except under the condition that he shall immediately become free, the owner of these slaves could not do it without involving himself in the same consequences."[56] Professor Paul Finkelman writes that the *Lemmon* case would have presented precisely the question that Justice Nelson said the Court was prepared to decide. "In reversing the New York Court of Appeals decision," Finkelman speculates, "the court could have taken the first step toward nationalizing slavery. The court could have found for Lemmon on two separate grounds: first, New York's statute was an unconstitutional interference with interstate commerce; second, the statute was also an abridgement of the comity guarantees of article IV."[57]

Can we fairly say that Lincoln demonstrated his case that there was a "tendency" toward the nationalization of slavery? As Jaffa pointed out, Lincoln was always careful to say that he "believed" it to be true that there was an unspoken conspiracy between the "four workmen." The evidence was circumstantial, but the niche that Lincoln predicted would be filled by *Dred Scott* was accurate. And his prediction of a "second *Dred Scott*" decision would certainly have been fulfilled had the Civil War not intervened. The Taney Court was ready and waiting, not only to complete the nationalization of slavery, but to deal a death blow to the Republican Party. This case was undoubtedly on its way to the Supreme Court and may have been the one to satisfy Justice Nelson's requirements for a decision to nationalize slavery. As Finkelman wrote in 2017, "it is likely that the *Lemmon* case would have reached the Court and led to the 'second *Dred Scott* decision' that Lincoln feared would nationalize slavery."[58]

Lincoln opposed the *Dred Scott* decision from the moment it was announced. In the first of many such accusations, Douglas, Lincoln's arch-nemesis, accused him of waging a "crusade against the Supreme court of the United States on account of the *Dred Scott* decision."[59] In the third Lincoln–Douglas debate, Douglas argued that "[i]t is the fundamental principle of the judiciary that its decisions are final. It is created for that purpose, so that when you cannot agree on a disputed point you appeal to the judicial tribunal which steps in and decides for you, and that decision is then binding on every good citizen. It is the law of the land just as much with Mr. Lincoln against it as for it."[60] Lincoln gave an extended reply in the sixth debate: "We oppose the *Dred Scott* decision in a certain way," Lincoln stated.

> We do not propose that when *Dred Scott* has been decided to be a slave by the court, we, as a mob, will decide

him to be free. We do not propose that, when any other one, or one thousand, shall be decided by that court to be slaves, we will in any violent way disturb the rights of property thus settled, but we nevertheless do oppose that decision as a political rule, which shall be binding on the voter, to vote for nobody who thinks it wrong, which shall be binding on the members of Congress or the President to favor no measure that does not actually concur with the principles of that decision . . . We propose so resisting it as to have it reversed if we can, and a new judicial rule established upon this subject.[61]

Thus, Lincoln's opposition was to the *Dred Scott* decision "as a political rule," to be overturned, if possible, by political means. In Lincoln's view, the decision was factually wrong, the product of a split court, and derived from no precedent. It was thus politically vulnerable, and Lincoln made a political issue of *Dred Scott*, eventually skewering Douglas on the contradiction between his advocacy of the "sacred right" of popular sovereignty—the right of local majorities to vote slavey "up or down"—and the Court's prohibition against voting slavery down because it deprived a slaveowner of his right to property.

One state case that Lincoln almost certainly did not know about demonstrated that the *Dred Scott* opinion was having an impact. The Supreme Court of California handed down a decision in the case of *Ex Parte Archy* in January 1858 that upheld a slaveowner's right to take his slave into the state even though the California Constitution banned slavery. Justice Peter H. Burnett, citing *Dred Scott*, noted that "[i]t must be concluded that where slavery exists, the right of property of the master in the slave must follow as a necessary incident.

The right of property is recognized by the Constitution of the United States. The right of property having been recognized by the supreme law, certain logical results must follow this recognition." Those "logical results" dictated that slave property must be protected as much as any other form of property and that "[n]o distinction can be made . . . between the different descriptions of private property." Thus, despite the fact that the California Constitution prohibited slavery, "in virtue of the paramount sovereignty of the United States, the citizens of each State have the right to pass through the other States, with *any* property whatever."[62]

The Dred Scott *Decision and the Republican Party*

Harry Jaffa has emphasized how politically charged the *Dred Scott* decision was. The events we have already described point to an effort on the part of the Supreme Court with the collusion[63] of both the executive and legislative branches to disable, if not destroy, the Republican Party. Jaffa notes that in 1858:

> The demand for the restoration of the Missouri Compromise slavery restriction was . . . the only real unifying force in the Republican party, the absolute sine qua non of its continued political existence. The election of 1856 had revealed that the Democratic party was now a minority party in the nation as far as the presidential vote was concerned. The Whig and Know-Nothing parties were breaking up rapidly, and it was highly probable that the Republican party would become the majority party in the not very distant future. The Republican party appeared to be on the threshold of overthrowing

the hegemony of the Democratic party, as neither the Federalists nor Whigs had ever threatened to do. The elections of 1856 carried the clear portent of an impending realignment of political strength in the nation, such as had not happened since 1800. And the decision in the case of *Dred Scott* coming hard on the heels of those portents, was a declaration that the election of a Republican administration would be election of a party dedicated to the overthrow of the Constitution—i.e., the Constitution as seen by Taney.[64]

Jaffa's conclusion was Lincoln's conclusion, but it was no less shocking: "The *Dred Scott* decision was nothing less than a summons to the Republicans to disband. . . . [I]t can hardly be doubted that the *Dred Scott* decision was the revolution in constitutional law Lincoln asserted it to be and that the acceptance of that decision as politically binding would have been as much an abnegation of the principles of popular government as were the doctrines of nullification and secession."[65] In fact, Taney's *Dred Scott* opinion might be most profitably read as a point-by-point refutation of the Republican Party platform of 1856.

It would be helpful here to review some of Lincoln's statements from the House Divided speech regarding the political character of the *Dred Scott* case. After President Pierce's pre-endorsement of the *Dred Scott* decision, he said the midterm election results of 1856 fell short of an outright approval of his endorsement by "nearly four hundred thousand votes [and] was not overwhelmingly reliable and satisfactory." In his last annual message, Pierce reiterated his endorsement: "The Supreme Court met again," Lincoln duly notes, and "*did not* announce their decision, but order[ed] a re-argument." And then, the "Presidential inauguration, and still no decision of the court." But the incoming President Buchanan, in "his inaugural address fervently exhorted the people to abide by the forthcoming decision, *whatever it might be*." Then, and only then, Lincoln recounts, the Supreme Court announced its decision. Then, and only then, Lincoln reiterates, the author of the Kansas-Nebraska Act, Stephen Douglas, endorsed the *Dred Scott* decision. We remember, of course, that the Republican Party at this time had only one reason for being: the repeal of the Kansas-Nebraska Act and the restoration of the Missouri Compromise. Here is the link between the *Dred Scott* decision and Taney's attempt to destroy the Republican Party!

On March 6, 1860, Lincoln delivered a remarkably candid speech at New Haven, Connecticut, in which he remarked that for the Republican Party the "question of Slavery" now "assumes an "overwhelming importance." "[I]n short," Lincoln says, "we think Slavery a great moral, social and political evil, tolerable only because, and so far as its actual existence makes it necessary to tolerate it, and that beyond that, it ought to be treated as wrong." "[I]n its political aspect, does anything," Lincoln queries, "in any way endanger the perpetuity of this Union but that single thing, Slavery? . . . Whatever endangered this Union, save and except Slavery?" Lincoln then poses a rigorous challenge: "Whenever this question shall be settled, it must be settled on some philosophical basis. No policy that does not rest upon some philosophical public opinion can be permanently maintained."[66] There are only two possibilities. Either slavery is right and "we must agree that Slavery is right" and "Slavery is morally right and social elevating." This would establish a "philosophical basis for a permanent policy of encouragement." The other policy is that slavery is wrong. Of course, the argument that slavery is "morally right" can have no philosophical basis because the idea that one man can ever be the property of another is irrational and therefore *contra natura*. Strictly speaking there can be no "philosophical public opinion." There can be public opinion, if guided by "enlightened statesmen," that coincides or rests on a philosophic basis without the public having a complete understanding of that philosophic basis. That would be the case of the "self-evident truth" of the Declaration that "all men are created equal" and its necessary concomitant that the "just powers" of government are derived from the "consent of the governed." These would be "true opinions" because the truth of these opinions rested on the "coincidence" of reason and revelation, those propositions which animated Lincoln and the founders.

Professor Diana Schaub has pointed out a little noticed biblical reference near the end of the *Dred Scott* speech. Lincoln, of course, had asserted, contrary to Chief Justice Taney and Senator Stephen Douglas, that the "the authors" of the Declaration clearly intended to include blacks in its central principle that "all men are created equal."[67] Douglas had appealed to northern racial prejudices by stoking fears of racial "amalgamation." Lincoln countered by suggesting that "the separation of the races in the only perfect preventive of amalgamation."[68] There is no doubt that "separation" would be a "perfect preventive," but was it practicable? Lincoln knew, of course, that the most practicable solution—but uncertain of immediate results—was "opposition to the spread of slavery."[69] Lincoln next spoke of colonization, as he did often. But for Lincoln, as for other statesmen, including Henry Clay, colonization served as a kind of rhetorical cover which allowed a principled stand against slavery to be indulged openly without shocking racial prejudices, because the promise of colonization was that freed slaves would be removed from any association with whites.[70] Lincoln, however, often expressed the sheer impossibility of colonization, mainly because of the expense involved, and the difficulty of convincing blacks to agree voluntarily. "Let us be brought to believe" Lincoln says, "it is morally right, and, at the same time, favorable to, or, at not against, our interest, to transfer the African to his native clime and we shall find a way to do it, however great the task may be."[71] It is at this point that the clause that Professor Schaub notes, suddenly appears: "The children of Israel, to such numbers as to include four hundred thousand fighting men, went out of Egyptian bondage in a body."[72] Lincoln seems to give this as proof that colonization is feasible when there is a will to do so. Professor Schaub rightly says that Lincoln must be referring to Exodus 12:37, but points out that the verses in Exodus speak "only of the number 'on foot that were men'. But describing men on foot as if they were foot soldiers and then highlighting these infantry men, Lincoln seems to be encouraging his white audience to be aware of how many fighting men there would be among the former slaves." In alluding to Exodus, Schaub claims that white America is cast in the role of the Egyptians and blacks in the role of "the children of Israel."[73] Thus the "new birth of freedom" announced in the Gettysburg Address would require a crisis—a punishment—and a salvation. The crisis was, of course, the Civil War, the salvation, as we have already seen, would be a republican regime based on the consent of the governed—all of the governed—without exception.[74]

Chapter Four

THE GETTYSBURG ADDRESS, BEGINNING AND END: EQUALITY AND LIBERTY

PARAGRAPH ONE:
THE PAST AS PROLOGUE

Harry Jaffa wrote, in language that itself deserves to be memorialized, that:

> The utterances that have come down to us, graven in bronze and in stone like the Gettysburg Address and the Second Inaugural, are profound meditations on human experience. In the midst of the horrors of destruction and death, and amid the turmoil of the passions of war, they are designed to reconcile us to our fate by discerning the hand of God in events that might otherwise seem merely chaotic. Although these speeches arise out of particular events at particular times, they draw back the curtain of eternity and allow us, as time-bound mortals, to glimpse a divine purpose within a sorrow-filled present, and tell us how our lives, however brief, can nonetheless serve a deathless end.[1]

The House Divided Speech, Jaffa argues, was meant to serve a different purpose, and as such, serves as a prelude to the Gettysburg Address, just as it served as a prelude to the Civil

War. "Of all Lincoln's speeches," Jaffa writes, "whether greater or lesser, the only one that can be said truly to have changed the course of history" was the House Divided Speech "delivered to the Republican State Convention in Springfield, Illinois, June 16, 1858." The House Divided Speech was "a causal agent in bringing about the terrible events over which Lincoln was destined to preside." A point of decision had been reached that was decisive—world changing—"because no middle ground existed any longer. That was Lincoln's message. The reason it *was* Lincoln's message was that Stephen A. Douglas, and his doctrine of popular sovereignty, seemed to offer that very middle ground whose existence Lincoln denied, a middle ground that influential Republicans were finding increasingly attractive."[2] In other words, the House Divided Speech was everything that the Gettysburg and Second Inaugural speeches were not, the rehearsal of arguments derived from particular facts and particular circumstances. Both later speeches were meditations on human nature—on the human soul.

Professor George Anastaplo, an accomplished exegete, and Lincoln scholar, wrote of the "lyrical compactness," the "sense of authority," and the "sublimity" of the Gettysburg Address. This made the speech appear to have been delivered "from a great height in intellect, time, and moral stature." All of this conspired to make the Gettysburg Address resemble "in its solemnity and pithiness the Lord's Prayer. And like that prayer, it begins with an invocation of the paternal and concludes with a vision of the ever after."[3] Indeed, I say, the Gettysburg Address is as close to a national prayer as the people of America of all religious sects and creeds are willing to accept.[4] Anastaplo notes that the familiar opening ("Four score and seven years ago our fathers. . .") "seems deliberately archaic" in a paragraph "which is itself devoted to the past." This "makes the interval since the founding of the Country seem longer than it really is, much more so than 'eighty-seven years' or even 'three generations' would have sounded. The language is not only archaic but (here as elsewhere) even Biblical in its connotations."[5] Indeed! Other writers have suggested the language of Psalm 90: "The days of our years are three score ten."[6]

The first paragraph of the Gettysburg Address is made up of one sentence, 30 words, and is the only paragraph devoted to the past. It also contains the most important theoretical precept in the entire speech, that "our fathers brought forth . . . a new nation, conceived in Liberty, and dedicated to the proposition that all men are created equal." Since this is the only paragraph dedicated to the past, it provokes the question of whether the *proposition* of equality has been relegated to the past, a question to be explored in short order. We also note parenthetically that the word "Liberty" is the only capitalized word in the speech (with the exception of God in the last paragraph). What it means to be "conceived in Liberty" also needs to be examined in some detail.

Before we begin a detailed examination of these questions, let us look at Anastaplo's outline of the speech as a whole. Anastaplo was a student of Leo Strauss and it might not be inappropriate to refer to his "outline" as a "Straussian geography" (although as a serious-minded scholar Anastaplo would probably have regarded this characterization as frivolous). In any case, Anastaplo notes that in the first paragraph a continent and a nation are mentioned; thus, the movement is from continent to nation. In the second paragraph, the movement is from nation to battlefield, and from battlefield to a "portion of that field." In this descent from a continent to a "portion of a battle-field," Anastaplo points out, the sentences get shorter and shorter down to the last sentence of paragraph two: "It is altogether fitting and proper that we should do this." "Then," Anastaplo observes, "the movement is reversed; from here to the end, there is an expansion of sentence lengths," commencing with the phrase "But, in a larger sense." Thereafter, Anastaplo rightly observes, "[t]he sentences get longer and longer . . . and [as] the scope of the vision becomes larger [Lincoln] moves from a 'portion of that field' to 'the earth.' The time with which he deals also expands, moving from 'four score and seven years' and the contest over whether this government 'can long endure' to the recitation of deeds that will never be forgotten and to the expression of the determination this government 'not perish from the earth.' This sense of expansion is reinforced by the final [sentence], the last of ten, which contains almost one-third of the entire address. This sentence, which marches steadily along, to the drumbeat of a high proportion of one- and two- syllable words, runs on and on, as if forever."[7] Overall, the geographical movement is from continent to earth. Neither the United States nor America is ever mentioned; of the fathers who brought forth the unnamed "new nation," nary a name is mentioned. It is a strange geography that contains no place names—even the word "cemetery" does not appear; and it is a strange history that does not mention the names of those who walked upon its stage. The speech thus seems to have no location—no fixed space. What is more, the fifth sentence, at the center of the speech, makes a promise that is unfulfilled. It promises "to dedicate a portion of that field . . ." But in the next line we are admonished that "we cannot dedicate. . ." What are we to make of this overly abstract document that seems to leave us in the middle of an uncharted ocean without a "sheet anchor?"[8]

Let us return to the beginning. We have already noted the Biblical allusion of the opening: "Four score and seven years ago. . ." Professor Diana Schaub lists the occasions that Lincoln referred to the birth of America: at Peoria he said, "Near eighty years ago we began by declaring that all men are created equal." On subsequent occasions, he mentioned 80 years, 81 years, "eighty-two years," "about eighty-two years," and "eighty-odd years."[9] Schaub asks:

> Why did he not continue his confirmed practice and begin the Gettysburg Address by saying 'Eighty-seven years ago'? Why this substitute: Four score and seven years ago'? Mathematically, of course, the two formulations are equivalent. Yet, he made his audience and all subsequent readers do a fair bit of arithmetic in order to puzzle out the date. . . . Four score (four times twenty) and seven (plus seven) equals eighty-seven years. The address was delivered in 1863, subtracting eighty-seven from 1863 takes you back to 1776. Note that either formulation (eighty-seven or four score and seven) requires knowledge of the date of the speech's delivery. Thus, it is not just 1776 that is commemorated. 1863 is enshrined forever as the minuend (the mathematical term for the part you start with before you take away the subtrahend). It is often said that Lincoln must have chosen his opening phrase because it sounded more poetic than the alternatives, but I must say it is an odd form of poetry that requires multiplication, addition, and subtraction. By the time the audience had performed the three operations to arrive at 1776, the speech would have been over.[10]

Thus, we may infer from Professor Schaub's account that what was dedicated at Gettysburg was not a "portion" of a battlefield, a cemetery, but a date—1863. As Professor Schaub demonstrated, the complicated arithmetic imposed upon the audience at the beginning, in a paragraph putatively dedicated to the past, forced the attention of the audience on the present and "enshrined forever" that date in their memories. Could that have been the principal focus of the dedication, to establish, as it were, an eternal present that encompasses past and future?

In *Crisis of the House Divided*, Harry Jaffa refers to the Gettysburg Address as one filled with "unsurpassed beauties." And so, it is! Jaffa remarks that: "The 'people' is no longer conceived in the Gettysburg Address, as it is in the Declaration of Independence, as a contractual union of individuals existing in a present; it is as well a union with ancestors and with posterity; it is organic and sacramental."[11] Jaffa continues with a detailed explanation of this last, intriguing phrase:

> For the central metaphor of the Gettysburg Address is that of birth and rebirth. And to be born again to Lincoln and his audience—as to any audience reared in the tradition of a civilization shaped by the Bible and by Plato's Republic—connoted the birth of the spirit as distinct from the flesh; it meant the birth resulting from the baptism or conversion of the soul. This new birth is not, as we have said, mere renewal of life but the origin of a higher life. Thus Lincoln, in the Civil War, above all in the Gettysburg Address and Second Inaugural, interpreted the war as a kind of blood for the baptism of the soul of a people.[12]

Much has been made of the fact that Lincoln refers to the central theoretical principle of the founding, that "all men are created equal," as a *"proposition"* in the Gettysburg Address. It has been vigorously argued by knowledgeable commentators that in Euclidean geometry a proposition is distinguished from a self-evident truth and that the appearance of the word "proposition" in the Gettysburg Address represents a development in Lincoln's political philosophy. Lincoln certainly knew the difference between a self-evident truth and a proposition in Euclidean geometry, since we learn from material supplied for a campaign biography in 1860 that he "studied and nearly mastered the Six-books of Euclid, since he was a member of Congress."[13] It is doubtful that there was any development of Lincoln's political thought between the Peoria Speech in 1854 and Gettysburg in 1863. The only development that occurred during that time was in how Lincoln determined the changing political climate dictated the rhetorical presentation of the principle of equality. This is always the challenge of republican statesmanship, since it must work withing the boundaries of consent which Lincoln said in the Peoria Speech, as previously noted, was the "sheet anchor of American republicanism." Consent, of course, means public opinion. Republican statesmanship must therefore work within the confines of public opinion, and its primary task is to direct public opinion to salutary and just ends, those ends, the purpose or telos, which the Gettysburg Address emphatically specifies are to be found in the Declaration. Harry Jaffa repeatedly argued that the secret to the Gettysburg Address was to understand the end in terms of the beginning and the beginning in terms of the end—Equality and Liberty.

In *Crisis of the House Divided*, Jaffa says that the time covered by the Lincoln–Douglas debates was "the 'prophetic period' of [Lincoln's] career, whose keynote was a return to ancestral ways." During this time, the "great central tenet" of the Declaration that "all men are created equal" became an "ancient faith." Thus, "in the Gettysburg Address, what was called a self-evident truth by Jefferson becomes in Lincoln's rhetoric an inheritance from 'our fathers.' This is not to suggest," Jaffa says, "that Lincoln doubted the evidence for the proposition," but it is quite possible that he found that it was more politically efficacious to describe the "four score and seven years" to reside more in the fact of its inheritance than in its accessibility to unassisted human reason. "The 1863 speech," Jaffa said, "tacitly obscures the rational foundations of the proposition to which it says the nation was dedicated."[14] Self-evident truths, of course, as we have previously discussed, can be defended on the basis of reason;[15] but the political efficacy of a self-evident truth is largely dependent upon public opinion. And in the Gettysburg Address, when Lincoln calculated the birth of the nation was in 1776, not 1787, he indicated that the "life blood" of the nation was the Declaration, not the Constitution. Lincoln accepted the Constitution and its compromises, which he regarded as necessary concessions when it came to the issue of slavery; but as Jaffa notes, "the central proposition of the Declaration was its final cause. It was common dedication to this which was the primary constituent element in our nationhood, and no change in the final cause was possible which would not destroy the nation so constituted. Lincoln's attitude toward the 'central idea' of American political public opinion . . . was also the central constitutive element of American nationality . . ."[16]

Jaffa, of course, was not unaware that four years before the Lincoln–Douglas debates, which he marks as the beginning of Lincoln's "prophetic period," Lincoln had said in the Peoria Address that "[n]ear eighty years ago we began by declaring that all men are created equal; but now from that beginning we have run down to the other declaration, that for SOME men to enslave OTHERS is a 'sacred right of self-government.'"[17] "Let us return . . . to the position our fathers gave it," Lincoln concluded, to "the earliest practice and precept of our ancient faith."[18] Jaffa was certainly aware of this passage in the Peoria Address, but apparently wanted to emphasize the more visible political aspects of the Lincoln–Douglas debates. Our interest here is Lincoln's mention of Douglas' "sacred right of self-government" which he believed was undermining the people's sense that slavery was a moral wrong by emphasizing that the question of slavery was only one of whose interests were being served. "This *declared* indifference," Lincoln said,

> but as I must think, covert *real* zeal for the spread of slavery, I can not but hate. I hate it because of the monstrous injustice of slavery itself. . . . and especially because it forces so many really good men amongst ourselves into an open war with the very fundamental principles of civil liberty—criticising the Declaration of Independence and insisting that there is no principle of action but *self-interest*.[19]

Douglas's policy of "squatter sovereignty" was that the majority of a territory or new state could decide the issue of slavery. If a majority decided it was in their interest to have slavery, then they would "vote it up," if not, they would "vote it down." Douglas frequently said he "don't care" which way the majority decided because in a democracy majority vote was sacred and no limits could restrain its decisions, whether they were motivated by justice or injustice. The interest of the majority was the only standard; justice was no part of the calculation. Lincoln, however, constantly pointed out that it was always in someone's interest to enslave others, whether the master of slaves, tyrants over an entire people who find it in their interest to do so, or those who used the argument of Divine Right of Kings to salve their consciences for their acts of tyranny. Douglas's argument would justify the enslavement, not only of blacks, but whites, and all human beings that "our ancient faith" once taught us were created equal.

I firmly believe that Jaffa never equivocates in *Crisis of the House Divided* that Lincoln always understood equality in the Declaration to be a proposition. Even when he spoke of it as a "self-evident truth," Lincoln, I say, understood the equality implied in that statement to be "aspirational,"—a proposition—something to be achieved, a goal or a guide, perhaps never realized, but an end or purpose—a telos inherent in human nature.

Lincoln's Dred Scott Speech, delivered at Springfield, Illinois on June 26, 1857, is the best example of his understanding of the Declaration as a proposition.[20] Lincoln took great pains to refute Chief Justice Taney's argument in *Dred Scott* that the Declaration's central tenet, that "all men are created equal," was not intended to include blacks of African descent. Taney, Lincoln says, "admits that the language of the Declaration is broad enough to include the whole human family, but he . . . argue[s] that the authors of that instrument did not intend to include negroes, by the fact that they did not at once, actually place them on an equality with the whites. Now this grave argument comes to just nothing at all, by the other fact, that they did not at once, *or ever afterwards*, actually place all white people on an equality one with another." Lincoln deftly points out the illogic of Taney's argument: on Taney's own supposition, he has "proven" that the Declaration did not include whites by the mere fact that not all whites were equalized all at once!

Lincoln continued:

> I think the authors of that notable instrument intended to
> include all men, but they did not intend to declare all men
> equal in all respects. They did not mean to say all men
> were equal in color, size, intellect, moral developments, or
> social capacity. They defined with tolerable distinctness, in
> what respects they did consider all men created equal—
> equal in 'certain inalienable rights, among which are life,
> liberty, and the pursuit of happiness.' This they said, and
> this meant. They did not mean to assert the obvious un-
> truth that all were then actually enjoying that equality,
> nor yet, that they were about to confer it immediately
> upon them. In fact they had no power to confer such a
> boon. They mean simply to declare the right, so that the
> enforcement of it might follow as fast as circumstances
> should permit. They meant to set up a standard maxim
> for free society, which should be familiar to all, and re-
> vered by all; constantly looked to, constantly labored for,
> even though never perfectly attained, constantly approx-
> imated, and thereby constantly spreading and deepening
> its influence, and augmenting the happiness and value of
> life to all people of all colors everywhere.[21]

Taney's argument wholly misunderstood the founders' view
of statesmanship. Lincoln argued that the "abstract truth" at
the core of the Declaration served no practical purpose in
effectuating independence from Great Britain. In fact, Lincoln says, it was not placed in the Declaration for that reason, but for future use, as a "standard maxim" or a goal to
be attained. Once it was accepted, the Declaration placed
moral demands on all Americans. How those demands were
to be met and at what speed had to be determined by wise

statesmen, and Lincoln's principle of statesmanship was that of the founders: eliminate as much evil as possible while it is possible without destroying the basis in public opinion from which further evil can be eliminated. In a regime based on the consent of the governed, statesmanship must always operate within the constraints of public opinion at the same time that it attempts to lead public opinion ever closer to the fulfillment of its highest aspirations.

Lincoln, of course, makes it abundantly clear that the equality of the Declaration must be understood in terms of natural right or "the rights of human nature," to use Madison's phrase. It is a self-evident truth that "all men are created equal" because no one is so superior by nature as to occupy the position of a natural ruler, having been marked by God or Nature's God to rule. It is also a self-evident truth, as we have previously argued, that "all men are not created equal in all respects." As Lincoln noted, men are not created "equal in color, size, intellect, moral developments, or social capacity." They are, however, created equal in the natural rights to "life, liberty and the pursuit of happiness."[22] None of the qualities in which men are created unequal establishes a claim to rule others by nature. Size or strength may give one the *power* to rule, but not the *right* to rule by nature.

Jaffa points out that Lincoln mounts his strongest argument for "the equality of natural rights of all human beings" in the case of a black woman's natural right to eat the bread that she has produced by her own hands, and observes that "Lincoln by implication invokes Locke's idea of the natural right of property as originating in that with which a man mixes his labor."[23] By invoking the natural right of a black woman, in the Dred Scott speech, Lincoln makes the strongest argument for the natural rights of all blacks. Jaffa makes an even stronger argument in his last formulation of the issue in *Crisis of the Strauss Divided* where he argues that "[a]lthough Lincoln is a political partisan in the Lincoln–Douglas debates, he brings into his analysis of the chief question dividing them—the morality of slavery—a perspective which is nothing less than that of political philosophy. When Lincoln said that a black woman had the same right as he himself, or Judge Douglas, or any other man, to put into her mouth the bread that her own hand had earned, he was invoking natural right—and the principle of natural equality—in their purest form. In doing so, he was appealing to distinctions rooted in the human condition, that transcend ancients and moderns, and that required no recasting by modern science."[24]

There is no doubt that Lincoln here, and throughout his career, believed that the Declaration supplied the end or purpose, the telos, for the Constitution, and that the Constitution was intended to put the principles of the Declaration into practice. But as in all things political, it is rarely possible to translate principles directly into practice. Insofar as the Constitution allowed the continued existence of slavery, it was an incomplete expression of the Declaration's principles. Madison argued that the compromises with slavery were necessary to secure the adoption of the Constitution—otherwise the slave-holding states would have bolted the Constitutional Convention.[25] And as the most thoughtful of the Federalists understood, without a strong national government the prospects of ever ending slavery were remote.[26] Thus the prudential compromises regarding slavery in the Constitution were actually in the service of eventual emancipation. As Lincoln always maintained, the Constitution, when understood in the light of the principles of the Declaration, put slavery "in the course of ultimate extinction."[27]

Those provisions in the Constitution protecting slavery were no part of the Constitution's principles; they were compromises designed to allow the ultimate fulfillment of the Constitution's principles. The Constitution treated slavery as in principle wrong—a necessary evil—to be tolerated only as long as necessary and to be eliminated as soon as politically possible. A compromise is not itself a principle but is often necessary for the implementation of principles. Slavery could not be abolished all at once, but the "public mind," according to Lincoln, had been convinced that slavery had been put on the course of ultimate extinction by the Constitution. Resist the spread of slavery by constitutional means and prepare the public mind for its eventual demise. This is republican statesmanship.

Chief Justice Taney's view is today fully endorsed by liberal academics and taught in almost every political science and history classroom: Since the founders did not eliminate slavery all at once, they never intended to eliminate slavery at all. This kind of categorical view was entirely alien to founders, and to all competent thinkers, except perhaps the most intransigent followers of Immanuel Kant. Since the founders did not eliminate all evil all at once, they never intended to eliminate any evil. Lincoln's Dred Scott Speech is the best antidote to this particular amoral way of thinking which makes the perfect the enemy of the good.[28] As Lincoln pointed out, the founders did not have the power to eliminate slavery all at once. The only possible way it could have been done was by tyrannical action, i.e., action not supported by the consent of the governed. In 1776 it was easy for the people to agree in principle that all men are created equal; but it was a different matter for them to consent to the abolition of slavery. Racial prejudice was a persistent fact. But the agreement in principle that "all men are created equal" was important. All deeds begin with a thought, and as Lincoln might have said, "the thought is the father of the deed" in the same way that he said that the principles of the Declaration were the father of all "moral principle" among us.[29] Once the thought is accepted—once the principle is accepted—then moral demands can be made to live up to the principles, and statesmanship becomes a matter of how those demands are to be met and at what speed. The telos or end supplied by Declaration is always the guide or goal—the proposition—even though the word itself doesn't always appear. Thus, in the Dred Scott Speech equality is understood, not as a "self-evident truth" which is not susceptible of further proof, but as if it were a proposition which needs further proof, an unfulfilled promise or aspiration, that must be developed or proven. That, I believe, was Lincoln's understanding of a proposition as it was Euclid's.

Eva Brann notes that in the Declaration of Independence the "principles, which mark the true beginnings of the nation" were held by "the fathers as *self-evident Truths*." But "[s]omething has happened between the founding and the [Gettysburg Address] which forces Lincoln to call the axioms of the Declaration mere propositions. This is what had happened," Brann ventures: "the Declaration had been called in public 'a self-evident lie,' a phrase Lincoln often cited with repugnance, for it creates a fatal situation." Brann then quotes the famous passage from a letter that Lincoln wrote to Henry L. Pierce and others, on April 6, 1859. I will quote more liberally from the letter than Brann does:

> But soberly, it is now no child's play to save the principles of Jefferson from total overthrow in this nation.
>
> One would start with great confidence that he could convince any sane child that the simpler propositions of

Euclid are true; but, nevertheless, he would fail, utterly, with one who should deny the definitions and axioms. The principles of Jefferson are the definitions and axioms of free society. And yet they are denied, and evaded, with no small show of success. One dashingly calls them 'glittering generalities'; another bluntly calls them 'self-evident lies'; and still others insidiously argue that they apply only to 'superior races.'[30]

Brann comments that Lincoln "understood that self-evidence is a peculiarly delicate affair, since when once impugned, once only denied in public, a self-evident truth turns into a debatable proposition. Yet, as the axiom, precisely by reason of its self-evidence, was unprovable, so the proposition has no rational proof from higher principles, but can be verified only from its consequences or—dreadful prospect—from the fatal consequences of its contrary."[31] Brann continues that this is the "peculiar danger of a nation which lives on a tradition of explicit principle rather than of ingrained myth. . ."[32] "Ingrained myth" is an unfortunate expression, but Brann is struggling here to find the phrase that Lincoln adopted in what we have seen Jaffa call his "prophetic period," namely that the principles the Declaration are our "ancient faith." How can we fail to see this as the best rhetorical antidote to the charge that the principles of the Declaration are a "self-evident" lie?

Brann's quotation of Lincoln's letter repeats his statement that "[t]he principles of Jefferson are the definitions and axioms of free society." Lincoln was steadfast in maintaining this statement, principally because Jefferson was "a chief actor in the revolution" as "the author of the Declaration of Independence."[33] Presumably we can conclude that Lincoln thought the principles of the Declaration were compatible with the "definitions and axioms of free society." We have previously discussed the first of Euclid's axioms that "things equal to the same thing are equal to each other" as the most compelling way to explain a "self-evident truth."[34] The "definitions" are more difficult to explain. The first is that "a point is that which has no part;" the second that "a line is breadthless length," i.e., a line has nether breadth nor length; and so on. But still the question remains: Are the "definitions and axioms of free society compatible with the definitions and axioms of Euclid? That is a more difficult question, but I say, that Lincoln believed they were, simply because, for Lincoln, it was always a political consideration, never a mathematical one. In other words, it was a matter of political efficacy, or to speak more precisely, a matter of political prudence, which, as we have argued all along, is the practical virtue that rules the human sphere as such.

How can we understand the curious proposition that "our fathers brought forth . . . a new nation, conceived in Liberty"? How can a "new nation" be "conceived in Liberty"? Notice that Lincoln did not say that our "fore-fathers brought forth" a "new nation." That would imply that the "new nation" was not "conceived in Liberty," but that it was entailed by the legacy of "fore-fathers." As it is, "conceived in Liberty" implies something unique, unprecedented, having a new beginning, created almost *ex nihilo*. Doesn't the speech as a whole appear to present something of an empty canvass awaiting the deft touches of a creative artist? This is certainly the thrust of Lincoln's famous pean to Jefferson in a Letter to Henry L. Pierce and others that he wrote in 1859 from which we quoted immediately above: "All honor to Jefferson," Lincoln noted,

> To the man who, in the concrete pressure of a struggle
> for national independence by a single people, had the
> coolness, forecast, and capacity to introduce into a mere-
> ly revolutionary document, an abstract truth, applicable
> to all men and all times, and so to embalm it there, that
> to-day, and in all coming days, it shall be a rebuke and
> a stumbling-block to the very harbingers of re-appearing
> tyranny and oppression.[35]

As a "merely revolutionary document," the Declaration of Independence would be unexceptional. It might represent the exchange of one set of rulers for another without any change in principle. This would be a "mere revolution": the exchange of one set of arbitrary rulers for another based on who could exercise the greatest force—or commit the greatest fraud. There would be no consideration of the common good or justice—or any bow in the direction of universal principle. Jefferson, however, had "the coolness, forecast, and capacity" to introduce an "abstract truth"—that "all men are created equal" as a dictate of the "Laws of Nature and Nature's God." This meant that, instead of a "mere revolution," the American Revolution became a revolution in world consciousness based on the idea that governments could be based on reason and principle and were not left to the vagaries of force and fraud. America was the first nation—the first experiment—based on the principle that the "consent of the governed" could be the active agency of republican government. Divine Right of Kings, the most successful example of force and fraud, held sway in the West for more than a thousand years. As we have seen Jaffa argue, Lincoln believed this was indistinguishable from slavery itself. From the founding of America, freedom of conscience and emancipation inevitably marched together, as the two freedoms were necessarily one.[36]

"Or fathers brought forth . . . a new nation, conceived in Liberty. . ." "Brought forth," as many have noted, is Biblical language for "birth;" "conceived in Liberty" might therefore suggest, using the language of Psalm 51:5, of being conceived in sin: "in sin did my mother conceive me." But Lincoln insists at Gettysburg that the nation was "conceived in Liberty," not in sin, although, one suspects that the two are not mutually exclusive, as in the case of sexual congress before marriage. In that case, the "new nation" would be "unlawful" both in terms of law and tradition. If so, that would mean that the kind of Liberty that attended the nation's birth was indeed perfect freedom, that the founders had the freedom to create for the first time in history a truly republican form of government based on the consent of the governed. It was a new beginning for political life and a revolutionary change of the grounds upon which political life rested. It would be, as Lincoln announced at the end of the speech, a "government of the people, by the people, for the people." It would derive from the people; the people would provide its active agency; and it would be for the benefit of the people. This would be the first nation compatible with the principles of human nature, divested of all traces of tyranny that had prevented the development of those virtues that grace human nature and the human soul. That is what our fathers brought forth on the earth, not out of love for their children, but in Liberty.[37]

Alexander Hamilton in the first *Federalist* made this extraordinarily bold remark:

> It has been frequently remarked that it seems to have been reserved to the people of this country, by their conduct and example, to decide the important question, whether societies of men are really capable or not of establishing good government from reflection and choice,

or whether they are forever destined to depend for their political constitutions on accident and force. If there be any truth in the remark, the crisis at which we are arrived may with propriety be regarded as the era in which that decision is to be made; and a wrong election of the part we shall act, in this view, deserve to be considered as the general misfortune of mankind.

As bold as this remark was intended to be, it contains many qualifications and reservations as befits the unveiling of a great experiment that will decide the fate of all mankind. Reflection and choice, of course, implies reason and natural right; accident and force implies force and fraud and the continuance of the thousand-year reign of the Divine Right of Kings. This was a revolutionary experiment testing whether governments can be based on the consent of the governed. It is always the same question: can natural right become political right or is that just the dream of utopian speculators?

PARAGRAPH TWO:
THE PRESENT, THE FUTURE, AND ETERNITY
Paragraph two of the Gettysburg Address contains four sentences and seventy-two words. If our analysis of the first paragraph has any truth to it, that the putative dedication to the past of "our fathers" transmogrified into a celebration of an "eternal present," then paragraph two is also dedicated to the present—the Civil War and the survival of the nation. But it is a "present" that points to the future; indeed, in its political implications it points to eternity.

"Now we are engaged in a great civil war . . ." "Now" is conspicuously the first word of the paragraph and "a great civil war" occupies the present. This might account for the unusual number of times the first-person plural "we" occurs in the paragraph. Those "who here gave their lives" are not exactly eclipsed, but they seem to be subsumed in "we the people." At the center of his "Message to Congress in Special Session" delivered to Congress on July 4, 1861, Lincoln states that the Civil War, already underway, but not yet declared by Congress, was "essentially a People's contest. On the side of the Union," he continued,

> it is a struggle for maintaining in the world, that form, and substance of government, whose leading object is, to elevate the condition of men—to lift artificial weights from all shoulders—to clear the paths of laudable pursuit for all—to afford all, an unfettered start, and a fair chance, in the race of life. Yielding to partial, and temporary departures, from necessity, this is the leading object of government for whose existence we contend.[38]

This was always Lincoln's view of the American founding, a vision that was, as Jaffa noted, to be perfected some two years later in the Gettysburg Address. The Declaration of Independence supplied the principles of the founding, the self-evident truth that "all men are created equal." It was this principle that lifted all "artificial weights from all shoulders," those of class, caste, race, color, and religion. The Constitution yielded "to partial, and temporary departures, from necessity." That was the regime that Lincoln defended and at Gettysburg it became something for which "we contend."

Lincoln concluded his July 4th remarks by making a crucial observation that he had made many times in adumbrating the work of the founders and which we have accordingly acknowledged on several previous occasions: "Our popular government has often been called an experiment. Two points in it, our people have already settled—the successful *estab-lishing*, and the successful *administering* of it. One still re-mains—its successful *maintenance* against a formidable [in-ternal] attempt to overthrow it."[39]

The Civil War is the test whether a nation "conceived in Liberty, and dedicated to the proposition that all men are cre-ated equal" "can long endure." That experiment which Ham-ilton announced would "decide the fate of mankind" at the founding was still not settled and had reached its ultimate challenge in civil war—in which the slave-holding states had decided that the experiment had been a failure. The venue of the Gettysburg Address "was a great battle-field of that war." "We have come to dedicate a portion of that field, as a final resting place for those who here gave their lives that that nation might live. It is altogether fitting and proper that that we should do this." It is fitting and proper only if those who died on this battlefield did so in a just cause, in the cause of natural right, in the defense of the principles of the Declara-tion of Independence.

Those who fight in unjust causes—for the preservation or expansion of empire or tyrannical government—do have their memories preserved in the annals of history. History books are filled with the actions and deeds of those who have committed unjust and brutal acts of conquest, and we celebrate these conquerors as heroes—Alexander, Caesar, Napoleon. But can it be said that their celebration is "fitting and proper?"

American government was an experiment, and that ex-periment has not been completed. It was the first attempt in history to establish non-tyrannical government. For Lincoln and the founders, as we have discussed, any government that is not based on the consent of the governed is slavery.

The slaveholding states had always seemed to recognize this, although its leaders, including Calhoun, struggled to articulate this recognition in any coherent way. Calhoun and his epigones, when they denounced the principles of the Declaration of Independence as "the most false and dangerous of all political ideas," ultimately declaring the founding principles celebrated in the Gettysburg Address as a "self-evident lie," meant that slavery, in one form or another, was an inherent part of political life. The American experiment had failed because, from the very beginning, its fundamental principles were wrong. Its failure was fated by some mysterious, quasi-dialectic of history.

As Hamilton wrote in the *Federalist*, the annals of history record no successful examples of republics. Republics, he observed, were unstable, perpetually vibrating between the extremes of anarchy and tyranny. The prospects of a successful American experiment were different because it was based on a "new science of politics," which had made its principal progress in modern times, mostly thanks to the work of Locke. Still, it was an experiment, and it was unknown whether it would succeed. But the fate of mankind was at stake; was it possible for mankind to be relieved from tyranny? Or was freedom reserved only for tyrants? To be determined by the American experiment was whether government could be grounded in the consent of the governed and whether the people could be self-governing with individual rights, or whether the dark ages of slavery—under whatever euphemism government was called—would continue. It was a noble cause, agitating the question of whether natural right could become political right.

If the American nation does not continue to live, the memories of those who fell at Gettysburg in the battle to preserve its existence will not survive. This was surely on Lincoln's mind when he began to speak the lines of the third paragraph.

The Past As Future

The third and final paragraph of the Gettysburg Address contains five sentences and one hundred and sixty-nine words. As previously mentioned, the first sentence of the third paragraph withdraws the promise of the second paragraph—that it is "fitting and proper" to "dedicate" "a portion" of the field. "But, in a larger sense, we can not dedicate. . ." Lincoln now proclaims. How is this a "larger sense?" Lincoln seems to say that the deeds of those who fell in battle have already consecrated the battlefield beyond anything that speech can do. The battlefield has already been consecrated! "My words are not needed," Lincoln might be saying, "I merely walk in the shade of those who preceded me on the glorious day of their triumph. What he did say is that their deeds were "far above our poor power to add or detract." Note that Lincoln did not say above "*my* poor power" but "*our* poor power." The next sentence, oft-quoted, is perhaps the most successful example of democratic rhetoric ever voiced: "The world will little note, nor long remember what we say here, but it can never forget what they did here." This is the central sentence of a paragraph that is notable, not only for the absence of the pronoun "I," but for the frequency of the first-person plural "we." (Lincoln does not use "I" anywhere in the entire speech).

Lincoln, of course, knew that deeds cannot speak for themselves, that unless someone chronicles the deeds—gives them life—they will be forgotten as soon as the eye witnesses themselves are gone. Lincoln knew that his speech—delivered with self-conscious irony—would engender fame and his fame would be reflected upon those who died on the battlefield. He knew that his masterfully crafted rhetoric would bring those who died in the great battle of Gettysburg back to life—resurrected, as it were—so that their lives would live in memory forever. But that would happen only if the nation survives and "shall not perish from the earth." "It is for us the living, rather, to be dedicated here to the unfinished work which they who fought here have thus far so nobly advanced." That unfinished work, "the great task remaining before us," is "that we here highly resolve that these dead shall not have died in vain—that this nation under God, shall have a new birth of freedom—and that government of the people, by the people, for the people, shall not perish from the earth."

Thus a "portion of that field" was not dedicated, but "us the living" were "dedicated here to the unfinished work" which those who fought here nobly advanced. The "cause" they advanced was that "this nation, under God, shall have a new birth of freedom." Thus, the living will be dedicated, "baptized" as it were, here today for "a new birth of freedom"—a resurrection. As we have discussed in previous chapters, governments can be derived from principles that are eternal, the Laws of Nature and Nature's God, but at the same time, nations need founders, a philosophic statesman or a *phronimos* who, knowing what is best by nature, can determine what is best under particular circumstances. The "enlightened statesmen" of the American founding, as we have discussed, decided to embark on a revolutionary experiment: a regime based on the consent of the governed. That experiment was challenged and *in extremis* at the time of the Gettysburg Address. The nation, Lincoln clearly believed, would survive only by a renewal or rebirth of that experiment; but it would require a refounding animated by entirely different motives than those of the founders, motives that are indifferent to—indeed contemptuous of—public recognition. Governments cannot be eternal, but the principles which animate just and free government can be. The Civil War was an effort to preserve "this nation, under God," but mostly, I say, it was an effort to preserve the principles that make just government possible, that those principles "shall not perish from the earth." Was it still possible for reason and revelation to be brought together, as they were at the founding, to be the twin pillars upon which the American *politeia* would continue to rest?

Have Those Principles Perished from the Earth?

Harry Jaffa often quoted Leo Strauss's statement from the opening paragraph of *Natural Right and History* that German thought had sometime in the 1930s abandoned "the idea of natural right" and by doing so had created the historical sense and "unqualified relativism." Jaffa pointed out that the historical sense and unqualified relativism migrated to America and became the basis for Progressivism. Strauss's famous statement was that "It would not be first time that a nation, defeated on the battlefield and, as it were, annihilated as a political being, has deprived its conquerors of the most sublime fruit of victory by imposing on them the yoke of its own thought."[40] Jaffa notes that Strauss, of course, had in mind the Third Reich when he made this observation. But Jaffa notes that "among its predecessors none was more conspicuous than the Confederacy, defeated on the battlefield in 1865 and also annihilated as a political being. Although the Union cause had prevailed, and chattel slavery was brought to an end, the principles of the Declaration of Independence, celebrated in the Gettysburg Address, were eclipsed almost immediately."[41]

Jaffa was eminently correct in pointing to Progressivism as the proximate cause. Progressivism was driven by the main forces of modernity—science and historicism. Science, of course, is incapable of defending itself as a moral discipline. Science has undoubtedly done much for the relief of the human estate, alleviating poverty and disease, among other things. But science cannot address the most important human and political questions—what is good? What is just? What is the best regime? What is moral? These are the questions that animated classical political philosophy, the philosophy of Plato and Aristotle. They became known as value questions and were said to be beyond the competence of science, which rested on the fact-value distinction, a distinction that was crucial to the progress of science. Its power over nature—its conquest of nature—would not have occurred without the distinction between facts and values. Mathematical physics, the heart of modern science, would not have developed without the fact-value distinction. But modern science without a ground in morality inevitably led to complications of great magnitude: power over nature without any sense of how to use the power justly or for the good. It is thus power without purpose. It was truly a bargain with the devil. It eventually led to what one prominent political philosopher described as "the self-destruction of reason."

Authoritative Progressive and liberal opinion today holds steadfastly to the scientific view that reason can tell us nothing about value questions; reason cannot decide between competing values or competing value systems because the post-modern world, shaped in large part by Progressivism, has led us to believe that reason itself is merely the epiphenomenon of sub-rational forces—either one's irrational passions, or one's race, one's ethnicity, one's sex, one's trans sex, or a host of other irrational factors. But as any competent student of history knows, reason is the basis of civilization, constitutionalism and the rule of law. How can we draw any other conclusion from our reading of Lincoln—and Harry Jaffa?

Lincoln's Annual Message to Congress, December 1, 1862

In the "Annual Message to Congress" sent to anxious members on December 1, 1862, almost a year before the Gettysburg Address, Lincoln addressed intractable problems that confronted the nation:

> Fellow-citizens, we cannot escape history. We of this Congress and this administration, will be remembered in spite of ourselves. No personal significance, or insignificance, can spare one or another of us. The fiery trial through which we pass, will light us down, in honor or dishonor, to the latest generation. We say we are for the Union. The world will not forget that we say this. We know how to save the Union. The world knows we do know how to save it. We—even we here—hold the power, and bear the responsibility. In giving freedom to the slave, we assure freedom to the free honorable alike in what we give, and what we preserve. We shall nobly save, or meanly lose, the last best, hope of earth. Other

means may succeed; this could not fail. This way is plain, peaceful, generous, just—a way which, if followed, the world will forever applaud, and God must forever bless.[42]

In the Preliminary Emancipation Proclamation issued on September 22, 1862, Lincoln indicated he would recommend to Congress on December 1 practical measures to implement compensated emancipation and colonization. Hardly anyone could have anticipated his proposal for three constitutional amendments to be practical under the circumstances that existed in December 1862. Did Lincoln's optimism cloud his sense of political reality? Did he misjudge political circumstances? Neither seems likely. Did Lincoln conceal his real intentions? The message is complex—and the peroration just quoted—is most striking.

The first constitutional amendment proposed by Lincoln specified that every state where slavery then existed that chose to abolish slavery, either immediately or gradually by January 1, 1900, would be compensated by the United States through the issuance of interest-bearing bonds. The second amendment guaranteed that all slaves who enjoyed "actual freedom" from the "chances of war" before the end of the rebellion "shall be forever free" and that loyal owners of slaves who have gained actual freedom would be compensated. The third proposed amendment would order Congress to appropriate funds to colonize "free colored persons" with their consent outside the United States.[43]

After introducing the amendments, Lincoln indulged a simple observation: "Without slavery the rebellion could never have existed; without slavery it could not continue." He also quoted his own words from the First Inaugural, illustrating that this simple observation teetered on the precipice of a great moral divide: "One section of our country believes slavery is *right*, and ought to be extended, while the other believes it is *wrong* and ought not be extended. This is the only substantial dispute." In Lincoln's mind the moral divide had been crossed—slavery was wrong and ought not to be extended. Emancipation and preservation of the Union had become inextricably bound together into one purpose. But could the people become reconciled to that purpose? Could Americans ever become one people, united once again by its ancient faith that "all men are created equal?" Reuniting the people would require sacrifices on both sides. There would be compensations for the sacrifices; but could the compensations be equal or even proportional? This would certainly be a requirement of justice.

The extended period allowed for compensated emancipation in Lincoln's proposed amendment (until January 1, 1900) would naturally disappoint those still bound to servitude because they would have no guarantee of immediate freedom or even prospects of freedom in their lifetime. But, Lincoln stressed, the lack of immediate freedom would be compensated by the knowledge that their posterity would enjoy freedom. By the same token, those who advocated perpetual slavery would be disappointed by the abolishment of slavery by compensated emancipation; but their disappointments would be mollified by the long grace period in which slavery would continue. The sacrifices, to say the obvious, are not equal or proportional. On the one hand, many slaves will never regain their freedom because of the extended grace period; on the other hand, the grudging sacrifice of slavery will be softened by compensation and a thirty-seven-year grace period: This simply does not balance on the scales of justice! It doesn't provide much common ground, but it would cause many sources for festering resentments on both sides that would, in all likelihood, extend well beyond thirty-seven years.

Masters and slaves would supposedly benefit from the fact that the status of both classes would not suddenly be disrupted by wholesale emancipation. Slaves would not be left destitute; masters would have time to become accustomed to the loss of their privileged status and the fact that they eventually would have to treat their former slaves as fellow citizens with privileges and immunities equal to their own. Yet surely this would not happen in thirty-seven years or in three generations. And the sacrifices demanded on the part of the two classes were grossly disproportional. Were they justified as "necessary evils"?

The money to pay for the compensation of slaves was to come from taxes paid by the people of both North and South. The people of the South, Lincoln argued, were no more responsible for introducing slavery into America that the people of the North. And the people of the North were not hesitant to use the products of slave labor imported from the South, so it is hardly accurate to say that the South had been more responsible for the continuance of slavery than the North. The injustice of slavery must be shared in common by the nation as a whole. Compensated emancipation was therefore a common object of the nation, and all sections should share the common charge associated with it. Making this a common cause, Lincoln apparently calculated, might help unify the nation, although this seemed to be a rather unrealistic hope in such a tumultuous time, and might well become yet another source of sectional resentments. The slaveocracy had ignored Lincoln's appeal to reason at the time of his First Inaugural; it was hardly expected that they would listen to him twenty-one months later when passions had elevated to an even greater pitch. The slaveocracy was still unable to listen to the voice of reason.

On December 8, 1863, Lincoln delivered his Annual Message to Congress. He proposed to extend to states a guarantee of a Republican Form of Government upon the tender of an oath of allegiance to the Constitution and the Union, and to the laws and proclamations regarding slavery. Lincoln continues that "while I remain in my present position I shall not attempt to retract or modify the emancipation proclamation; nor shall I return to slavery any person who is free by the terms of the proclamation, or by any of the acts of Congress." "The suggestion in the proclamation as to maintaining the political framework of the States, Lincoln concluded, "on what is called reconstruction, is made in the hope that it may do good without danger of harm. It will save labor and avoid great confusion."**

Harry Jaffa Unmasks a Leading Progressive Historian

Harry Jaffa wrote an extensive commentary on Carl Becker's *The Declaration of Independence: A Study of the History of Political Ideas*, first published in 1922 and still regarded the

---

**   It was pointed out to me by me by Julie Ponzi that it is important to note that Lincoln says "what is *called* reconstruction." He does not ever say "reconstruction" without some qualification, simply to forestall the idea that secession can ever be thought constitutional or that there had ever been an actual breach of the Union. Ponzi described it perfectly in this language: "To speak of reconstruction concedes the fact of deconstruction."

authoritative work on the Declaration. Becker was a leading Progressive historian, and his brand of historicism dominates history and political science departments yet today. Jaffa points out that the core thesis of his influential work on the Declaration is that "[t]o ask whether the natural rights philosophy of the Declaration of Independence is true of false is essentially a meaningless question."[44] Jaffa cogently counters "if the question as to whether the philosophy of the Declaration is true or false is essentially meaningless, then questions as to whether slavery is right or wrong or whether freedom is better than despotism are equally meaningless."[45] Jaffa addresses the crucial question of whether the historical school has in fact refuted the "natural rights philosophy" of the Declaration.

The "historical school" claimed to have challenged natural rights philosophy on its own ground and refuted it on its own premises. Conceding that natural rights might be found in nature, Jaffa writes, "it identified nature with history and affirmed that institutions of any nation were its experience, the résumé of its history." This implied, Jaffa continues "that every people has, therefore, at any given time, the social order which nature has given it, the order which is on the whole is best suited to its peculiar genius and circumstance . . ."[46]

Jaffa's critique of the "historical school's refutation" is devastating: "The idea of nature as a standard" in the natural rights philosophy "is the idea of an unchanging ground of changing experience. To identify nature with history is to identify the unchanging with the changing or to alter the meaning of nature into its opposite. This is a substitution of meanings, not a refutation. A refutation would have to take the form of a demonstration," Jaffa continues, "that there is no unchanging ground of human experience." In my considered opinion, Jaffa rightly concludes that there has never been such a demonstration. "The most that can be said for Becker," Jaffa asserts, "is that he assumes that since the dominant philosophical schools have gone from nature to history as the ground of understanding and judgment, they must have done so for a sufficient reason. In that he is simply mistaken."[47]

In the simplest terms, Jaffa has revealed that Becker's final insight into the "truth" of history is that "all truth" is relative to the historical conditions that produced it. We will not be so boorish to ask how Becker's insight, which was a product of his own historical epoch, can be valid for *all historical epochs*. It is difficult to imagine that Becker did not recognize the logical self-contradiction at the center of his own insight. Yet, beyond all reason, Becker's view is the one that dominates departments of history and political science. Even though it is based on an unproven—indeed unsustainable—premise, it has nevertheless become the unquestioned orthodoxy in virtually all disciplines in the social sciences—think only if the many mandatory courses in "Race and Racism." All students are taught that values are relative and are merely the result of "social construction." There are no superior or inferior values; the only distinction between values and value systems is the intensity with which they are held. Nature or natural right has been expelled from the universe of the Progressives—and today's universities—and replaced by "historical consciousness."

Some final reflections on the prudence of Lincoln's statesmanship will bring this chapter on the Gettysburg Address to a conclusion. Attentive readers will recognize that this theme has been present throughout for the simple reason that prudence has always been a part of American statesmanship.

It was enshrined in the Declaration of Independence itself. Harry Jaffa's latest discoveries demonstrate that the concept of prudence, properly understood in terms of book five of Aristotle's *Ethics*, informs the Declaration and is immune to the imaginary barrier that has been erected between ancients and moderns. Prudence as understood by Aristotle and the American founders informed Lincoln's statesmanship. Prudence is the virtue at the heart of political life—it is a practical and a theoretical virtue. Aristotle's *phronimoi*, having reflected on what is simply best, know how to apply what is possible under a variety of circumstances. Politics sometimes presents intractable problems from the point of view of justice, as we saw when Lincoln was confronted with the issue of post-war reconciliation on the issue of slavery. Perfect justice is rarely possible and expectations, especially in a regime based on consent, will cause resentments that will tend to dislocate and undermine political life. The greatest danger is to the rule of law. This is the danger that Lincoln spoke about in the Lyceum Speech in 1838, that the toleration of injustice, whether necessary or not, will encourage the lawless in spirit and those who tolerate the lawless in spirit, to undermine the rule of law and the faith in the principles that support the rule of law.

Lincoln, of course, was never an abolitionist because the abolitionists would have ignored the Constitution and the rule of law to achieve what they thought was a just result—pure abolition. *Fiat justitia ruat caelum!* This, of course, disregarded the extent to which the Constitution and the rule of law were essential to a just result. Kant's *Perpetual Peace* contained a similar statement of what amounted to a categorical imperative. But the categorical imperative has never been part of American justice.[48] Prudence has always been at the center. Prudence is essential to political justice; and natural right is a *part* of political justice. Lincoln was acutely aware that prudence was the virtue that was at the center of political life—it was essential to republican freedom. The slaveocracy shared the same apocalyptical view of politics as the abolitionists. "A new birth of freedom"—"under God"— the final message of the Gettysburg Address required a restoration of prudence.

Chapter Five

THE SECOND INAUGURAL AND A RETROSPECTIVE ON THE FUTURE, OR, A "SUMMING UP" OF SORTS

Several years ago I made a discovery about Abraham Lincoln's First Inaugural that confirmed my long-held conviction that he crafted his works with extraordinary care. The speech begins with the ordinary observation that "in compliance with a custom as old as the government itself, I appear before you . . . " The address begins with custom or convention. Turning to the end of the speech, I found, to my surprise, the word "nature." The speech begins with custom and ends with nature. This, of course, reminded me of Socratic dialectic, the attempt to elicit truth by beginning with custom or opinion and ascending to nature or natural right. The theme of the First Inaugural is unquestionably an appeal to reason. The slaveocracy has no cause to leave the Union—leaving simply does not advance its interests. This discovery led me to examine the beginning and end of the Second Inaugural.

The Second Inaugural begins with "At this second appearance to take this oath" and ends with peace among nations ("a lasting peace, among ourselves, and with all nations."). Thus, the First Inaugural represents an appeal to Reason whereas the second represents an appeal to Revelation.[1] This is precisely where we left the Gettysburg Address: the rebirth of a nation to recapture its original foundations, those foundations resting on the twin pillars of Reason and Revelation.

There has been some desultory speculation as to whether Lincoln actually chose the last words of the First Inaugural or whether "better angels of our nature" was dictated by Secretary of State-designate William Seward. Michael Burlingame reports that Seward had considerable success in persuading Lincoln to temper his remarks about sectional conflict, but that over-all his influence was modest. As to the final paragraph, Lincoln read Seward's suggestions, and no doubt took them seriously, but completely rewrote them, always ensuring through the various drafts that the phrase "the better angels of our nature" ended the paragraph. Burlingame suggests the phrase "'better Angel' occurs in Dicken's *David Copperfield*."[2] Professor Diana Schaub, a literary critic of some note, has called Seward's suggestions for "a more poetic ending" a "flatfooted version" that had to be "reworked by Lincoln."[3]

The Second Inaugural
(four paragraphs, twenty-five sentences, 701 words.)

In one of the many pithy remarks that grace his works, Harry Jaffa observes "[t]he somber theology of Lincoln's second inaugural address . . . is the epitaph of the utopian belief in progress that so dominated the mid-nineteenth century."[4] In what seems to be merely an off-hand comment, Jaffa also reveals that "Lincoln's fascination with *Macbeth* is clearly due to its theme of the relationship of wrongdoing and retribution, and the kinship with his own second inaugural is obvious."[5] We mentioned in the introduction to this book that Jaffa considered the connection between *Macbeth* and *Hamlet* to be the key to understanding not only Lincoln's biblical understanding but also his understanding of Shakespeare, the two sources Lincoln said were his inspirations for politics. As we have remarked throughout, Lincoln always understood prudence to be at the core of political life, a lesson he traced to the Declaration of Independence.

Several scholars have pointed out that the immediate source of Lincoln's Second Inaugural was Thomas Jefferson's *Notes on the State of Virginia,*[6] where Jefferson, in a solemn passage that deserves to be quoted *in extenso* wrote,

> can the liberties of a nation be thought secure when we have removed their only firm basis, a conviction in the minds of the people that these liberties are of the gift of God? That they are not to be violated but with his wrath? Indeed I tremble for my country when I reflect that God is just: that his justice cannot sleep for ever: that considering numbers, nature and natural means only, a revolution of the wheel of fortune, an exchange of situation, is among possible events: that it may become probable by supernatural interference! The Almighty has no attribute which can take side with us in such a contest —But it is impossible to be temperate and to pursue this subject through the various consideration of policy, of morals, of history natural and civil. We must be contented to hope they will force their way into every one's mind. I think a change already perceptible, since the origin of the present revolution.[7]

Jefferson asserts God's justice, venturing that the "liberties of a nation"—the "gift of God"—cannot be violated without provoking his "wrath." Jefferson claims that it is impossible "to be temperate" when pursuing this subject. When he speaks of God's "wrath," we have no doubt that Jefferson means something severe—something terrible. But, unlike Lincoln in the Second Inaugural, Jefferson cites no biblical passages to bolster his point. He does say, however, that God's justice "cannot sleep for ever." While he again gives no biblical support, he does put forward a natural explanation: "considering numbers, nature and natural means only, a revolution of the wheel of fortune, an exchange of situation, is among possible events: that it may become probable by supernatural interference. The Almighty has no attribute which can take side with us in such a contest." Natural processes, working themselves out, independently of God's plan, will cause a revolution of the wheel of fortune that cannot impel God to take the side of the white race in what will likely be a race-war. It will, however, provoke God's "supernatural interference." This is the familiar confluence of "Nature and of Nature's God."

The question is, can slave masters be persuaded by reasonable arguments to emancipate their slaves? Jefferson asserts we "must be contented to hope" that considerations of policy, morals, and history, both natural and civil, will work to influence slaveholders. Jefferson says, "we must be contented to hope," but we know that revolution was never very far from Jefferson's thinking, especially in these early days. We quoted Jaffa in an earlier chapter noting that Jefferson only accepted elections as a successor to revolution as a control on government in the election of 1800. And in the *Notes*, revolution is always on prominent display.

Since Jefferson continues to claim that slavery is not a subject that encourages or inspires temperance, the thought behind Jefferson's statement here is unquestionably that the nation cannot continue to survive divided between the principles of the Declaration of Independence and the continued existence of slavery. The nation must become all free or all slave. It cannot remain divided. This is the true origin of the House Divided theme—the nation must become all free, according to the principles of the Declaration, or all slave. As Lincoln will argue in his House Divided Speech and ultimately in the Gettysburg Address, there is no ground for compromise between slavery and freedom. There is no principle that can accommodate both.

Jefferson even anticipates something that resembles Hegel's master-slave dialectic. "I think a change already perceptible," Jefferson says, "since the origin of the present revolution. The spirit of the master is abating, that of the slave rising from the dust, his condition mollifying, the way I hope preparing under the auspices of heaven, for a total emancipation."[8] In Jefferson's case, however, the "dialectic" doesn't seem to be inevitable! It will depend on wise statesmanship. No one understood this better than Lincoln.

FIRST PARAGRAPH
(FIVE SENTENCES, 130 WORDS)
The first paragraph of the Second Inaugural deals with the present, the war, and Lincoln makes no predictions about the future although the end of the war in terms of the "progress of our arms" is entirely predictable. What is not predictable is whether the American people can be reunited after the war has ended.

We have already noted the beginning of the Second

Inaugural: "At this second appearing to take the oath of the presidential office . . ." The newly elected president is required by the Constitution to take an "Oath or Affirmation" which obliges the president to "preserve, protect and defend the Constitution of the United States." There is no requirement that the newly elected president make an inaugural address, even though he is required to give Congress information on the state of the union and recommend considerations for measures he shall judge necessary and expedient. There is no requirement, however, that this requirement be fulfilled by what has become the "State of the Union Address."

We have already pointed out Lincoln's opening remarks at his First Inaugural where he characterized his appearance as a "custom" thereby indicating it was not compelled by law. The Second Inaugural is a "second appearing," which reminds us of the biblical Second Coming, although Lincoln surely would not claim his second appearance to be miraculous. Yet Lincoln's intention undoubtedly was to remind us of that miraculous event and the necessity of reading the end of the speech in the light of the beginning and the beginning in the light of the end.

Lincoln begins by remarking that this second appearance presents less occasion for an extended address than the first. For the First Inaugural it "seemed fitting and proper" that a detailed account of the course to be pursued should be given. We recall the phrase "fitting and proper" from the Gettysburg Address where Lincoln said it was "altogether fitting and proper" that we "dedicate a portion of that field, as a final resting place for those who here gave their lives that . . . the nation might live." Thus, Lincoln in the Second Inaugural succeeds in linking together the Gettysburg Address, the First Inaugural, and the Second Inaugural as "altogether fitting and proper." Fitting and proper, of course, means the speeches were right for the occasions, *prudent* endeavors to apply the abiding principles of justice to changing circumstances. The Second Inaugural seeks to prepare the American people to receive God's justice for the sin of slavery.

SECOND PARAGRAPH
(FIVE SENTENCES, NINETY-EIGHT WORDS)

The second paragraph focuses on the past; it goes back four years to the First Inaugural "when all thoughts were anxiously directed" to an impending civil war. Lincoln alleges that "all sought to avoid it." This, of course, is hyperbole, since the Southern sympathizers sought to avoid it by subverting the government by insurgency. That would avoid war but would destroy the government. Lincoln's First Inaugural was an attempt to *save* the Union by an appeal to reason as a way of subverting war. Perhaps the slaveocracy could be persuaded to remain in the Union. Would they listen? We remember Jefferson's attempts to convince slave masters to free their slaves by the mild voice of reason. Passion in Jefferson's time and in Lincoln's made the slaveholders deaf to reason. Those deaf to reason "would *make* war rather than let the nation survive; and the other [side] would *accept* war rather than let it perish. And the war came." In the First Inaugural, Lincoln argued that as a practical matter sovereignty rested, not with the states, but with the consent of the governed. This was the active agency of all legitimate government. The present crisis which will eventuate in Civil War is a fundamental moral and political question: "One section of our country believes slavery is *right*, and ought to be extended, while the other believes it is *wrong* and ought not to be extended. This is the only substantial dispute."[9] What is the proper way of deciding this question in a republic? "A majority," Lincoln replies, "held in restraint by constitutional checks, and limitations, and always changing easily, with deliberate changes of popular opinions and sentiments, is the only true sovereign of a free people. Whoever rejects it, does of necessity, fly to anarchy or to despotism."[10] Lincoln had earlier explained that "the central idea of secession, is the essence of anarchy." Any dissatisfied minority (or individual) can use the idea as a legitimate precedent for secession. The centripetal force set in motion, of course, would almost inevitably lead to anarchy. Since we know from experience that anarchy is unsustainable; it always leads to despotism, since in the state of nature the "war of all against all" forces everyone to fly into the arms of Leviathan.

In the last paragraph of the First Inaugural, Lincoln pronounces these famous words: "I am loath to close." Lincoln, I believe, knew that his attempt to persuade the South would be a failure. The slaveocracy was beyond reason. He knew that as soon as he stopped speaking, the war would come. No matter how long he might continue speaking, he could not forestall it—"And the war came." It was once again the eternal question: Can natural right ever become political right?

The first paragraph of the Second Inaugural addresses "the great contest which still absorbs the attention, and engrosses the energies of the nation." Lincoln says that he can present little that is new. "The progress of our arms is as well known to the public as to myself." Lincoln, of course, knows more of the "progress" of arms than the public because much about the movement of troops, supplies, and other details of tactics and strategy must be kept from the public eye. It seems, however, that everyone agrees that the progress of arms is satisfactory. Lincoln makes no predictions, although he knows that the victories of Sherman and Grant have effectually ended the war in spite of no surrender having yet been proffered. Lincoln could have safely predicted a victory in arms; but he could not predict whether the American people could be reunited. It was not the "progress of our arms" that preoccupied Lincoln in the Second Inaugural, but Reconstruction. That was the great "unpredictable" because the fundamental cause of the war, as we learn in the third paragraph, was deeper than slavery.

THIRD PARAGRAPH
(FOURTEEN SENTENCES, 393 WORDS)

The third paragraph is the longest. It addresses the question of the causes of the war and delves into the remote past for an answer. The short answer: slavery! But it is more complicated.

One eighth the population were "colored slaves" concentrated in "the Southern part" of the Union when the war came. These slaves constituted a "peculiar and powerful interest." "All know" that this interest was the cause of the war. The insurgents, Lincoln recounts, would "rend the Union" to extend the slave interest; the government would do no more than restrict its territorial extension. Both sides expected an easier triumph. Given James Buchanan's reaction to secession, that it was unconstitutional, but the federal government had no power to stop it, it is not surprising that the slavocracy did not expect the "magnitude or duration" of the war. Lincoln was certainly correct—after Buchanan's desultory performance, the South did not expect Lincoln's strong and decisive reaction—no Hamlet-like indecision stopped Lincoln's defense of the Union.

At the center of the paragraph, Lincoln reveals the real cause of the war: Everyone knew the slave interest was the cause of the war. Both sides sought to promote their respective interests by prayer: "Both read the same Bible, and pray to the same God; and each invokes His aid against the other. It may seem strange that any men should dare to ask a just God's assistance in wringing their bread from the sweat of other men's faces; but let us judge not that we be not judged. The prayers of both could not be answered; that of neither has been answered fully. The Almighty has His own purposes."

Here is the theological problem in its pristine form. Both sides read the same Bible, both sides pray to the same God; one side expects an unjust result, the other a just result. We have already seen Lincoln use the example of "wringing" bread "from the sweat of other men's faces" as the prime example of a violation of natural right—a violation of a slave's right to "self-ownership" which rests at the foundation of the idea of natural rights and the consent of the governed. A just God cannot approve an unjust result and this violation of natural right is palpably unjust.

But Lincoln, referring to Matthew 7:1, warns that we cannot judge because we will be judged in return. God does not reveal everything. We can't know which side will prevail in this terrible war. We know that God is just! But we know from experience that injustice exists in the world. How can a just God allow injustice to exist? What appears to us as injustice, however, may in God's plan or purpose, be just. We cannot know God's ultimate purpose; He works in mysterious ways. He reveals as much of his plan as He wishes us to know; but the rest He reserves for Himself, to be Revealed when He chooses. "Judge not lest ye be judged," is the only pious posture that can be assumed before such a mysterious God. We know that "wringing the bread from the sweat of other men's faces" is unjust; reason and nature reveal as much. But God allows slavery to continue. Why? It serves God's ultimate purpose, which we do not know but which we have faith will serve the ultimate cause of justice. God, we believe, cannot allow the injustice of the slavery we witness to exist except in the cause of justice.

If God was responsible for the creation of evil that would imply imperfection in the Creator, and we know—or at least our faith tells us—that God is a perfect Being. We simply cannot judge because we don't understand completely God's ultimate plan, and any judgement we make might bear false witness. That is why we are admonished not to judge. "The Almighty has His own purposes" is the great mystery which serves as the reasonable faith in justice that rests at the foundation of Western Civilization.

Where Jefferson ventures that liberties—the "gift of God"—can be violated only with the "wrath" of God, Lincoln says that the "Almighty has His own purposes" and supports this with a quote from Matthew 18:7. "Woe unto the world because of offences! For it must needs be that offences come; but woe to that man by whom the offence cometh!" Nothing is said in the Matthew passage about God's justice, only that woe will come. Lincoln refers to another biblical passage, this time from the Old Testament, Psalm 19:9. "The judgments of the Lord, are true and righteous altogether." The previous line, not quoted by Lincoln is revealing: these judgments emanate from "the fear of the Lord." We are obliged to note that they do not emanate from His love.

The next sentence in paragraph three (twelfth sentence) is the longest (seventy eight words), most complicated, most abstruse, and most mysterious of the entire speech.

> If we shall suppose that American Slavery is one of those
> offenses which, in the providence of God, must needs

come, but which having continued through His appointed time, He now wills to remove, and that He gives to
both North and South, this terrible war, as the woe due
to those by whom the offence came, shall we discern
therein any departure from those divine attributes which
the believers in a Living God always ascribe to Him?

Lincoln, of course, read the King James Bible, and the translation of Matthew 18:7 it presents is considerably more force-
ful than the Greek original. *Thayer's Greek-English Dictionary
of the New Testament* suggests that "woes" (οὐαί) are, as used
in Matthew, "an interjection of grief or of denunciation," such
as "alas!" or "woe!" and that that "offenses" (σκανδάλων) are
simply "enticements to sin." What Lincoln read in his Bible
was more expressive, I say, of what he intended the punishment to be visited upon the American people for their offenses. This is the biblical passage Jefferson would have cited in
the *Notes* had he been inclined to do so.

Professor Schaub rightly points out that this complex
paragraph is tentative or "experimental," beginning as it does
with "If we shall suppose . . ." Schaub suggests that Lincoln
recognizes how dangerous it is to mix religion and politics
and wants to introduce an element of uncertainty to prevent
extremism and "fanaticism" that often accompanies the use
of religion for political purposes. This explanation seems a
bit fanciful for someone who understands the theological-
political question as well as Lincoln does. It is true, however,
as Schaub observes, that Lincoln, at this point in the speech,
wants "to encourage humility rather than pride or certain-
ty."[11] This, of course, is part of Lincoln's understanding of the
theological-political question!

Professor Schaub gives what I think is the best summary

of the King James translation of Matthew 18:7 which Lincoln read: "Simply put, the war is the blood price the nation must pay for the sin of slavery."[12] Lincoln mentions "American Slavery" as one of the offenses. We notice the use of capitals. American Slavery means both North and South. We have visited this theme before. Both sides have profited from slavery, and both should pay for its sins—it is not a sectional issue. Lincoln is thinking of reunification and Reconstruction. But he is thinking of more than that.

America is unique in the sense that it is dedicated to a universal principle that all men are created equal. We have quoted Lincoln's apostrophe to Jefferson: "All honor to Jefferson . . ." It was a celebration of America's uniqueness, the fact that it was dedicated to a universal principle that "all men are created equal." We have discussed Lincoln's interpretation of this principle as a "standard maxim," a guide or goal (a) *telos* to be emulated, perhaps never achieved, but an end or purpose by which progress could be gauged. This was the ground of the great American Experiment launched by the founders and now judged to be a failure by the South.

If American Slavery is one of the offenses, which all must admit is the case, that "in the providence of God, must needs come, but which, having continued through His appointed time, He now wills to remove, and that He gives to both North and South, this terrible war, as the woe due to those by whom the offence came, shall we discern therein any departure from those divine attributes which the believers in a Living God always ascribe to Him." American Slavery *is* one of the offenses, and we believe, according to Matthew that "woe" will come to those who offended, both in the North and the South. But we don't know whether "this terrible war" has continued through "His appointed time." "Shall we discern therein any departure from those divine attributes which the believers in a Living God always ascribe to Him?" Presumably "those divine attributes" are omnipotence, omniscience, and, as we have just learned, mysteriousness.

The thirteenth sentence of paragraph three is a prayer, a prayer for mercy with a poetic rhyme. "Fondly do we hope—fervently do we pray—that this mighty scourge of war may speedily pass away." This is the prayer to a Living God to intervene on the side of righteousness and justice. Show us our faith is justified, Lincoln asks, and extend mercy to a suffering nation. Nearly two and one-half years before the Second Inaugural, Lincoln wrote some notes on theology that were published in *The Collected Works* as "Meditation on the Divine Will."[13] In this "Meditation," Lincoln mused that "[t]he will of God prevails. In great contests each party claims to act in accordance with the will of God. Both *may* be, and one *must* be wrong. God can not be *for*, and *against* the same thing at the same time." We note in passing that this is a "logical" or "mathematical" test of God's will that may ignore the possibility of the "miraculous," thus possibly denying God's omnipotence. But we shall not insist on this point. "In the present civil war," Lincoln continues, "it is quite possible that God's purpose is something different from the purpose of either party . . . He could give the final victory to either side any day. Yet the contest proceeds." The fact that both sides of this terrible war pray to the same God and read the same Bible means that there are sectarian disputes within Christianity. In some real sense this is a sectarian quarrel. Both sides use biblical exegesis to argue for or against the justice of slavery. Harry Jaffa remarks that "[t]he Civil War was as much a war between differing versions of Christianity (or about the teaching of the Bible) as it was about slavery and the Constitution. The division between the Northern churches and the Southern churches may be compared to the division between Protestants and Catholics in the wars of the Reformation."[14] "Whether Christianity condemned or endorsed slavery," Jaffa continued, "was one of the great issues that divided Americans on the eve of the Civil War. Because the Northern and Southern churches divided over the question, the Civil War took on many of the characteristics of a religious war."[15]

The fourteenth sentence of paragraph three considers that God may not answer the prayer of sentence thirteen that the war swiftly pass away. "Yet, if God wills that [the war] continue, until all the wealth piled by the bond-man's two hundred and fifty years of unrequited toil shall be sunk, and until every drop of blood drawn with the lash, shall be paid by another drawn with the sword, as was said three thousand years ago, so still it must be said 'the judgments of the Lord, are true and righteous altogether.'" The biblical passage quoted here is Psalm 19:9:

> The fear of the LORD is clean, enduring forever.
> The judgments of The LORD are true and righteous altogether.

Professor Schaub draws attention to Lincoln's use of the word "bond-man" in Lincoln's speech. This term, she reports, "is used repeatedly in the King James version of Deuteronomy to remind the Hebrews of their deliverance. . . . . If Blacks are analogous to the children of Israel, then the United States is the Pharaoh, whom God smites. Lincoln had warned of this parallel between American and 'Egyptian bondage' once before, at the conclusion of his *Dred Scott* speech."[16] We presume that the 250 years is Lincoln's approximate date of the first arrival of British settlers to America and the 3000 years ago would be the traditional date of Psalms. If "the judg-ments of the Lord, are true and righteous altogether," then all the compromises to allow the continued existence of slavery both before and after the American founding, whether by necessity or not, will be condemned and the blood drawn by the lash will be requited by blood drawn by the sword. Equi-ty driven by prudence will no longer be a part of the calculus. Necessity can no longer be proffered as an excuse! That was part of the sinful past that must now be paid in blood.

Lincoln's four biblical references in the Second Inaugural, Genesis 3:19; Matthew 7:1; Matthew 18:7; and Psalms 19:9, ac-cording to Professor Schaub, make it possible to understand the meaning in the last paragraph of "human charity, or at least a lessening of human malice. In other words," Schaub insightfully concludes, "Lincoln's theological interpretation has a political postwar purpose."[17] "[L]et us strive to finish the work we are in," Lincoln admonishes. We remember that at the Gettysburg Address Lincoln called on "us the living . . . to be dedicated here to unfinished work which they who fought here . . . so nobly advanced . . . that this nation, under God, shall have a new birth of freedom . . . " But this new work will involve the cultivation of a Christian virtue, charity and the suppression of the enemy of charity, malice. Charity is not merely the absence of malice, but "care"—"charity" and "care" and to "cherish a lasting peace." Will this be sufficient to "bind up the nation's wounds?"—not only of those who "have borne the battle," but "his widow, and his orphan." There is no celebration of victory here, either express or im-plied—that would not be charitable; it would be malicious because it would not heal sectional wounds. There is also no sense that peace will be magnanimous, because that implies generosity on the part of the victors. In this war there are

no victors, only victims who suffer the wrath of God equally for the sin of slavery. This must be a "just, and a lasting
peace, among ourselves, and with all nations." We have already discussed the intractable problems that are involved in
the construction of a "just and lasting peace" in the discussion of Lincoln's December 1863 message to Congress when
he presented three constitutional amendments designed to
end slavery by compensated emancipation. Full justice to
the "bond-man" was *impossible* and the punishment for the
slaveowner, in the scale of justice, however justice was measured, not severe enough. This was proof, as Lincoln always
knew, that America is Pharoah! That is the overwhelming
message of the Second Inaugural.

In the Introduction to this book, I related a conversation
I had with Harry Jaffa about Shakespeare's political genius.
Jaffa said that it was revealed most clearly in the connection
between *Hamlet* and *Macbeth*, which he thought showed
Shakespeare to be the Platonic poet envisaged at the end of
the *Symposium*. Most importantly for our purposes was the
realization that these two plays were at the center of Lincoln's
understanding of politics and that both plays are essential to
understanding the Second Inaugural. (See Appendix.)

A Retrospective on the Future: A "Summing Up" of Sorts

As previously mentioned, Lincoln's restoration of the founding and the principles of natural right was short lived, over-
whelmed by historicism, the central tenet of Progressivism.
This issue was discussed in chapter one and chapter four.
Our issue here is the extent to which reason is no longer a
part of public discourse—simply put, it has been expelled

by the proverbial pitchfork of historicism. But this time, it is unlikely that nature or natural right can force its return.

Passion renders reason incapable of being heard. This is the same situation that existed prior to the Civil War when Lincoln's appeal to the South to listen to reason was rejected. The moral question of whether slavery was right or wrong was not heard. We are repeating the same thing today. We have already heard a leading Progressive historian announce that the question of whether all men are created equal is true or false is meaningless. By logical parity, this implies that Lincoln is meaningless, since his very being was constituted by a dedication to the truth of that proposition. And, so the epigones of Progressivism have, in effect, denied the very existence of Lincoln as they attempt to deny a past that doesn't conform to their current "narrative."

Narrative has replaced history in an attempt to destroy the past and exaggerate the importance of the future. This goes beyond the shameful removal of Lincoln's statues and images from public view but extends especially to the moral obloquy that is unjustly heaped upon him because he was not an abolitionist or a follower of Kant's categorial imperative. The infamous "1619 Project," for example, wrote the history of black America without the slightest regard for historical truth. As with all Progressive-inspired projects, the "1619 Project" of the *New York Times* was not concerned with the past or present but the "end of history"—the future. The radical superiority of the future is guaranteed by the dialectic of history and any memory of the past (or the present) detracts from the illusion of the superiority of the future. "History" is thus malleable and exists to serve as "propaganda" for a future state. Narrative allows the judicious selection of facts that support a predetermined outcome that can be "validated" only in the future. In other words, historical truth is the first casualty of narrative which turns the reality of the present into the malleable utopia of the future. Does this sound familiar?

In the Civil War, the South was defeated on the battlefield, but in the Second Inaugural no victory was declared or implied; an olive branch was offered, and charity extended. In response, the South was offended and continued to defend the morality of slavery. "Who is to say that slavery is wrong and immoral?" the public asks today—and not just the South. It is a meaningless question because it is a value question! If slavery is not immoral, then we can say that nothing is immoral. Everyone is entitled to his own morality; when nothing is forbidden, everything is permitted, the state of nature—where everyone has an equal right to enforce the law of nature—is ever-present and never more-so than today. No amount of bluster about the superiority of the future will change the brutality of that fact. We do not expect a war of religion, but rather tribal wars, with new tribal gods, that will demand new sacrifices likely to be shocking in their level of brutality.

When the Civil Rights Act of 1964 was passed, almost every supporter of constitutionalism and the rule of law seemed optimistic that the final vestiges of race consciousness had been removed from the laws of the nation. It seemed to be the culmination of a long campaign to banish race, color, and ethnicity from the law. Its purpose was noble, and its reach was extensive—a belated victory for Abraham Lincoln and the principles of the Declaration of Independence. The dream of a color-blind Constitution had at long last been recognized, if perhaps not fully realized. The Civil Rights Act, along with the Voting Rights Act, passed the next year, had finally put the destructive genie of race securely in its bottle; there were now legal remedies available for racial injustices. But as soon as that old racial genie had been secured, new prophets arose and said: "We can teach that old genie new tricks. We can teach him to give up his evil ways and be a force for good. We will turn him loose to do the work of racial reparations and racial equity." Others with longer memories and further vision warned: "Don't do it! That evil genie is incapable of learning new ways; history has proven that he will always be a force for evil. He is a trickster. He will promise good things; he will promise equality, but he will never be satisfied with equality under the law. He always seeks superiority; he wants to rule; he wants to dominate; he will destroy. Don't let him loose again. You will regret it. That evil genie is willing to work every deception on those of good will, and in the name of equality he will destroy equal protection of the laws and racial equality." Have not these words of warning proven correct?

The narrative claiming that Lincoln was a "racist" is an utter outrage to any reasonable human being. But the hysteria that drives narratives leads to this incredible statement: "Because Lincoln was white, he must have been a racist." This is an unfounded assertion, not reason or logic. Perhaps the whole idea of the American founding that a regime could be based on "universal principle" and could govern itself by "deliberation and choice" put too much demand on the human capacity for reason. Perhaps human nature was incapable of living up to such high standards.

When I say, "All lives matter," I am called a racist! But when I ask my Black Lives Matter friends, "Why it is racist to say such a thing? The answer is always, "Because it is racist to say so." When I respond, "Since black lives are included in all lives, along with every other imaginable race or ethnicity, how can it be racist?" the answer is the same: "That is racist, too." "But" I persist, "the statement 'all lives matter' is a colorblind statement; how can it be racist?" Here I hit on the core of the problem. "Black Lives Matter" is itself an assertion of privilege, a statement of racial superiority. "All lives matter" suggests subordination of "black lives" in "all lives." Although it is a logically correct proposition that black lives are included in "all lives," it doesn't give black lives preeminence. Now we can understand why Western logic is "racist." It doesn't credit simple assertions of racial superiority.

Were equality and equal protection all along a utopian dream? Do people prefer privilege to equality? Do they desire to rule? Did the evil genie understand something that I didn't—or something that I thought could be overcome? Perhaps equality itself inspires both the desire to rule and the desire for privilege. If everyone is equal, then everyone is equally a ruler and has an equal right to rule. Why should the egalitarian impulse to rule be suppressed by a social compact that imposes obligations enforceable by government even if it is based on reason and consent? The narrative of consent is met by a narrative that was led in the form of a tricky rhyme by the Reverend Jesse Jackson some years ago at a protest rally against Stanford University's requirement that students take courses in Western Civilization: "Hey Hey, Ho Ho, Western Civ has got to go." This was something that may have been taught to the Reverend by our "reformed" trickster friend who had been recently released to perform charitable works. Reverend Jackson didn't say this, but he must have been aware that his chant extended to more than the course work at Stanford University and included Western Civilization as a whole. After all, wasn't it a settled matter that Western Civilization was the source of white colonialism and slavery?

How did our trickster friend know that the Reverend's chant would be so appealing? Because it had a tricky rhyme? As a chant it has a tribal charm? Was it a sufficient negation of Western reason? Our trickster has shown vastly greater sophistication and seriousness with his "black lives" appeal; he has seen how easily his charm and guile work. Our trickster may soon prophesize new gods, and if so, these new gods are certain to demand new sacrifices. Our trickster may even have read Heidegger!

It was the dedication to a universal principle that "all men are created equal" that became the foundation of America. It has been bandied about and widely accepted at the highest levels of government and education that this is simply an expression of "white supremacy." Its negation (or cancelation) will require some form of non-universal thinking—if that is possible. More likely its negation or cancelation will rest on simple assertion or some test of ideological purity that resembles tribal belief more than it does reasoned discourse, which it has rejected in advance. It won't be easy to destroy Western reason. It can't be done by reason or logic (or even ideology)—it must be done by force or mere assertion. I will not give up because I know for certain that tribalism is the worst of all possible forms of social organization, for within it, justice is left out of public discourse, since justice requires reasoned discourse! The founders and Lincoln were not racists. Our future—to the extent that we have a future—is with the founders and Lincoln, and with the Fourteenth Amendment's restoration of the principles of the founding. It is this vision—not "narrative"—that will pierce the gloomy darkness of impending tyranny.[18]

APPENDIX

On August 17, 1863, Abraham Lincoln wrote to James H. Hackett, a famous Shakespearean actor, complimenting him on his presentation of Falstaff that he had seen "last winter or spring." "Some of Shakespeare's plays," Lincoln continued, "I have never read; while others I have gone over perhaps as frequently as any unprofessional reader. Among the latter are Lear, Richard Third, Henry Eighth, Hamlet, and especially Macbeth. I think nothing equals Macbeth. It is wonderful. Unlike gentlemen of the profession, I think the soliloquy in Hamlet commencing 'O, my offence is rank' surpasses that commencing 'To be, or not to be.' But pardon this small attempt at criticism."[1] Almost exactly three months later, November 19, 1863, Lincoln delivered the Gettysburg Address.

Harry Jaffa also quoted the Hackett letter in *A New Birth of Freedom*, adding that "Lincoln's fascination with *Macbeth* is clearly due to its theme of the relationship of wrongdoing and retribution, and the kinship with his own second inaugural is obvious."[2] I believe that Lincoln prefers Claudius's soliloquy in *Hamlet* for the same reason. In the Peoria Address Lincoln compared the moral sin of slavery with obvious allusions to *Macbeth*:

> [Douglas] commenced by stating I had assumed all the way through that the principle of the Nebraska bill, would have the effect of extending slavery. He denied that this was intended, or that this effect would follow.

> I will not re-open the argument upon this point. That
> such was the intention, the world believed at the start,
> and will continue to believe. This was the countenance
> of the thing; and, both friends and enemies, instantly
> recognized it as such. That countenance can not now be
> changed by argument. You can as easily argue the color
> out of the negroes' skin. Like the "bloody hand" you may
> wash it, and wash it, the red witness of guilt still sticks,
> and stares horribly at you.[3]

Jaffa was less interested in pursuing Lincoln's declaration in the Hackett letter that he preferred Claudius's soliloquy to Hamlet's than he was in pursuing Lincoln's mention of the Henry plays.

Lincoln's conversations about *Macbeth* on April 9, 1865, after his visit to Richmond have been noted often. Steaming up the Potomac aboard the *River Queen* on his return to Washington, Lincoln was understandably in a somber mood even though he had learned that the War had been won, although no surrender had yet been tendered. The War had been a great trial by fire, and rivers of blood had been shed on both sides as punishment for the original sin of slavery. That was certainly the tone and tenor of the Second Inaugural! The Marquis de Chambru, a foreign dignitary, had accompanied Lincoln and reported that on the return trip his "conversation dwelt upon literary subjects. Mr. Lincoln read to us for several hours passages taken from Shakespeare. Most of them were from 'Macbeth', and, in particular, the verses which follow *Duncan's* assassination. I cannot recall this reading without being awed at the remembrance, when *Macbeth* becomes king after the murder of *Duncan*, he falls prey to the most horrible torments of mind. Either he was struck by the weird beauty of these verses, or from a vague presentiment coming over him, Mr. Lincoln paused here while reading, and began to explain to us how true a description of the murderer that one was; when, the dark deed achieved, its tortured perpetrator came to envy the sleep of his victim; and he read over again the same scene." The envy of sleep, of course, reminds us of nothing so much as the first part Hamlet's soliloquy (III.1.60–65).[4] In Lincoln's mind, *Macbeth* and *Hamlet* are always paired. Along the way Lincoln must surely have learned that it was *Macbeth* that taught him the meaning of tyranny, and perhaps this was one of his thoughts that day on the Potomac.[5]

Why do I mention all of this? Is there any real connection between the Hackett letter and the Gettysburg Address? I begin by mentioning that Lincoln had quoted from *Hamlet* in the Peoria Speech. Speaking of Stephen Douglas's "squatter sovereignty" policy in the Kansas-Nebraska Act as a compromise to solve the question of slavery by appealing to the unfettered interest of majorities, Lincoln said:

> Much as I hate slavery, I would consent to the extension of it rather than see the Union dissolved, just as I would consent to any great evil, to avoid a greater one. But when I go to Union saving, I must believe, at least, that the means I employ has some adaptation to the end. To my mind, Nebraska has no such adaptation
> "It hath no relish of salvation in it."
> It is an aggravation, rather, of the only one thing which ever endangers the Union.[6]

The soliloquy in Hamlet beginning "O, my offense is rank," is spoken by King Claudius, the usurping King of Denmark, who has murdered his brother, the legitimate king, and entered into an incestuous marriage with his widow, Hamlet's mother. Hamlet has solemnly sworn to exact revenge for these misbegotten and unholy deeds before the ghost of his father.

Claudius seeks to pray, but finds that he cannot:

> Though inclination be as sharp as will,
> My stronger guilt defeats my strong intent.

The reason? His offense

> hath the primal eldest curse upon't,
> A brother's murder.

The curse of Cain! This is an unpardonable sin. Besides, if the sin were perchance to be pardoned, all

> those effects for which I did the murder,
> My crown, mine own ambition, and my queen,
> May one be pardoned and retain th' offense?
> In the corrupted currents of this world Offense's gilded
> hand may shove by justice,
> And oft 'tis seen the wicked prize itself
> Buys out the law. But tis not so above,
> There is no shuffling; there the action lies
> In his true nature, and we ourselves compelled,
> Even to the teeth and forehead of our faults,
> To give in evidence. What then? What rests?
> Try what repentance can. What can it not?
> Yet what can it when one cannot repent?
> O wretched state! O bosom black as death!
> O limed soul, that struggling to be free
> Art more engaged! Help, angels! Make assay.
> Bow, stubborn knees,
> and, heart with strings of steel,

Be soft as sinews of the newborn babe.

All may be well. [He kneels]

This is a tyrant's prayer; it is fraudulent. It does not ask for salvation, only that judgment be postponed so that this-worldly "effects" can continue, and final judgment postponed. Along the way, there are allusions to *Macbeth*: "this cursed hand" thick "with brother's blood" and not enough water "To wash it white as snow." His ambitions urged on by Hamlet's mother almost speak for themselves.

We are reminded of Thomas Hobbes's argument in *Leviathan* that the fear of violent death has a more immediate and palpable influence on the souls of citizens than the remote and uncertain eternal punishment promised by God's representatives. The rational and calculating soul will hold dear the real goods of this world and refuse to exchange them for the imaginary goods of the next world. According to Hobbes (who obviously follows Machiavelli) immediate gains have a greater hold on men's souls than the promised but uncertain future salvation.

Claudius is Machiavellian. He will not gamble his real-world gains on the promise of future salvation, especially since he knows that there is no prospect of salvation for his "primal crime." Lincoln's interest in Claudius's soliloquy should be obvious. The only salvation for the original sin of slavery, regardless of how the blame for its origin may be parceled out, requires a new birth and a baptism of blood. The Civil War would be that baptism and the expiation of that original sin.

At this point, Hamlet makes his entry and sees Claudius kneeling and believes him to be praying. Claudius appears to be easily vulnerable to an assassination attempt. This is

Hamlet's opportunity to fulfill his promise and avenge his father. But, unlike a son hell-bent on revenge, Hamlet pauses to reflect: "If his prayers are answered, and he is in a state of grace, I will only hasten him to heaven." His act will therefore not be an act of revenge, but one of "hire and salary." Then

> Up, sword, and know thou a more horrid hent.
> When he is drunk asleep, or in his rage,
> Or in th' incestuous pleasure of his bed,
> At game a-swearing, or about some act
> That has no relish of salvation in't—
> Then trip him, that his heels may kick at heaven,
> And that his soul may be as damned and black
> As hell, whereto it goes. My mother stays.
> This physic but prolongs thy sickly day.

Hamlet's hesitation to act shows his unfitness to rule. He cannot be a king, although he has apparently acquitted himself as warrior. His simpleminded belief that his assassination of Claudius would send him heavenward in a state of grace—his Christianity—makes it questionable whether he can ever be a ruler. This is a contest between a pagan warrior—a Machiavellian—who knowing that his redemption is impossible, doesn't venture the impossible, and a Christian warrior who hesitates to execute at the decisive moment. Hamlet may have been the legitimate heir to Denmark, but he was incapable of rule; would the fulfillment of his promise to his father have proven his capacity to rule Denmark?

We thus end this digression where we began, with the Peoria Address: "That has no relish of salvation in't."

ACKNOWLEDGMENTS

Thomas Klingenstein, chairman of the board of directors of the Claremont Institute, and Ryan Williams, Chief Executive Officer of the Claremont Institute, supported this publication with resources and encouragement. I owe a debt of gratitude to both of these fine gentlemen in precisely the way Abraham Lincoln understood gratitude. Professor Scot Zentner, Chair of the Department of Political Science Department at California State University, San Bernardino, read and made comments on the entire manuscript. He saved me from an embarrassing mistake in the Introduction. Professor Brian Janiskee, past-chair and member of the same department, read and made interesting and helpful comments on the whole manuscript. Ken Masugi, Georgetown University and Hillsdale College, a long-time reader of my manuscripts, read the Introduction and the first two chapters, offered concise criticisms, especially about the meaning of δύναμιν in the Introduction. David Sonenstein, esq., who has assisted me in my previous publications, was helpful in interpreting biblical passages. He translated the Hebrew of Old Testament passages and checked the accuracy of the King James Bible that was used by Lincoln and reported that the King James Bible was a quite literal translation. Professor Daniel Palm, of Azuza Pacific University, was essential in helping me understand certain New Testament passages. Mark A. Schreckengost, Jr., a former student of mine at California State University (B.A., M.A.) and now a teacher at University

Preparatory at Victorville, California, listened to many hours of my readings of the manuscript and commented on many of the passages. This was truly heroic work on his part and I owe him many thanks for a job well done.

ENDNOTES

Introduction

1   Harry V. Jaffa, "The Unity of Tragedy, Comedy, and History: An Interpretation of the Shakespearean Universe," in John Alvis and Thomas G. West, eds., *Shakespeare as Political Thinker* (Durham, N.C.: Carolina Academic Press, 1981), 277–303.

2   *See* Harry V. Jaffa, "Equality, Liberty, Wisdom, Morality, and Consent in the Idea of Political Freedom," in Edward J. Erler and Ken Masugi, eds., *The Rediscovery of America: Essays by Harry V. Jaffa on the New Birth of Politics* (Lanham, Md.: Rowman and Littlefield, 2012), 11–46; *especially* appendix, 40–45. Originally published in *Interpretation: A Journal of Political Philosophy*, vol. 15, no. 1 (Jan. 1987).

3   "Thomas Aquinas Meets Thomas Jefferson," in Erler and Masugi, eds., *The Rediscovery of America*, 265–274. Originally published in *Interpretation: A Journal of Political Philosophy*, vol. 33, no. 2 (Spring, 2006).

4   "New Introduction" to the Claremont Institute edition of *Thomism and Aristotelianism*, forthcoming.

5   Harry V. Jaffa, *Crisis of the Strauss Divided*, 225–26. Jaffa showed that he could select whimsical titles for books, "Crisis of the Strauss Divided" being a frivolous play on "Crisis of the House Divided" suggested by one of his former students, herself a noted political philosopher. Jaffa

also "selected" chapter 17 for the placement of his essay "Too Good to be True?" in which he demonstrated that Aquinas, Jefferson, Washington, and Lincoln engaged in non-historicist thought. The number 17 for those who follow such things was the "classical" number for philosophy. Jaffa was whimsical and serious. Although the title of the chapter is not enclosed in quotation marks, I am almost certain it is taken from a phrase used by Professor Charles R. Kesler in his essay, "A New Birth of Freedom: Harry V. Jaffa and the Study of America," in Kenneth L. Deutsch and John A. Murley, eds., *Leo Strauss, the Straussians, and the American Regime* (Lanham, Md.: Rowman and Littlefield, 1999), 273. Commenting on Jaffa's account of the Lyceum Speech regarding Lincoln's presentation of the men of superior talents and abilities (those who belong to the "family of the lion or the tribe of the eagle") Kesler says "[e]xtreme human inequality and fundamental human equality were both true. This result may itself seem either too good to be true—a '*political truth*' is hardly the whole truth—or too true to be good, insofar as it appears to sideline all human virtue that fell short of the godlike. But Jaffa's point was that it was impossible to do justice to human equality and to human inequality at the same time in politics" (emphasis original). Jaffa was determined to refute Kesler's point that "it was impossible to do justice to human equality and to human inequality at the same time in politics." I believe Jaffa's account of Lincoln's Aristotelian statesmanship succeeded in doing so.

6   Jaffa, *Crisis of the Strauss Divided*, 21.

7   *See* footnote 2 above.

8   Jaffa, "Aristotle and Locke in the American Founding," in Erler and Masugi, eds., *The Rediscovery of America*, 6

(reprinted from the *Claremont Review of Books*, vol. 1, no. 2 (Winter, 2001).

Chapter 1

1 Michael P. Zuckert, "Jaffa's *New Birth*: Harry Jaffa at Ninety," in Harry v. Jaffa, *Crisis of the Strauss Divided: Essays on Leo Strauss and Straussianism, East and West* (Lanham, Md.: Rowman and Littlefield, 2012), 242. (First published in *The Review of Politics*, vol. 71 (2009), 207–223.

2 Harry V. Jaffa, "Equality, Liberty, Wisdom, Morality, and Consent in the Idea of Political Freedom," in Edward J. Erler and Ken Masugi, eds., *The Rediscovery of America: Essays by Harry V. Jaffa on the New Birth of Politics* (Lanham, Md.: Rowman and Littlefield, 2019), 13–45. (*Especially appendix*, 40–45). (Originally published in in *Interpretation: A Journal of Political Philosophy*, vol. 15, no. 1 (Jan. 1987).

3 Zuckert is particularly concerned about this statement, remarking that "Jaffa's idea of history as a text constructed with logographic necessity" was "most definitely" not understood by Strauss in that way "and Lincoln either fails to identify history with providence (*most of the time*) or, as in the Second Inaugural, identifies history with an unfathomable providence." Zuckert, "Jaffa's *New Birth*," at 244 (emphasis added). In a "Letter to Albert G. Hodges," April 4, 1864, in Roy P. Basler ed., *Collected Works of Abraham Lincoln* (Rutgers, N.J.: Rutgers University Press, 1953), VII.281, Lincoln explained a change in war policy concerning slavery: "I am naturally anti-slavery. If slavery is not wrong, nothing is wrong. . . . And I aver that, to this day, I have done no official act in mere deference to my abstract judgment and feeling on slavery. . . . [M]y oath to preserve the Constitution to the best of my ability, imposed on me the

duty of preserving, by every indispensable means, that government—that nation—of which that constitution was the organic law. . . . I felt that measures, otherwise unconstitutional, might become lawful, by becoming indispensable to the preservation of the constitution, through the preservation of the nation. Right or wrong, I assumed this ground, and now avow it. . . . *I claim not to have controlled events, but confess plainly that events have controlled me*" (emphasis added). No one but the most obtuse can fail to see the irony of this statement. Yet some (Zuckert?) take it at face value. *See* David Donald, *Lincoln* (London: Jonathan Cape, 1995), 514. The topic of Lincoln, history, and providence will be explored in greater detail in subsequent chapters. When Lincoln says he is "naturally anti-slavery," he undoubtedly means it is against natural right; the preservation of the "anti-slavery" constitution is also consistent with the principles of natural right, however much it may be inconsistent with legal or positive right. Lincoln, on his own initiative, has just changed the nation's war policy concerning slavery by violating the Constitution as he understood it, while at the same time saying he has not controlled events!

4 Ibid.

5 Ibid.

6 Harry V. Jaffa, "The Legacy of Leo Strauss," in *Crisis of the Strauss Divided*, 58–9.

7 Harry V. Jaffa, *American Conservatism and the American Founding* (Durham, N.C.: Carolina Academic Press, 1984), 138 (the epigraphs to *Natural Right and History* are "lucid examples of the necessity of natural right").

8 Harry V. Jaffa, "Strauss at 100," in *Crisis of the Strauss Divided*, 187.

9 Stephen A. Douglas, "Remarks of the Hon. Stephen A.

Endnotes

Douglas," Delivered at the State House in Springfield, June 12, 1857, 9–10 (emphasis added) (reprinted from *Cong. Globe*, 34th Cong., 1st Sess. (June 9, 1856), 1369–75.

10 Abraham Lincoln, "Speech at Chicago, Illinois," July 10, 1858, in *Collected Works*, 499–500. *See* Jaffa, *A New Birth of Freedom*, 146–152 (Ch. 2); 447.

11 "Straussian Geography," in *Crisis of the Strauss Divided*, 12.

12 Ibid., 30–31,

13 Jaffa, *A New Birth of Freedom*, 118–119. *See* 104.

14 Ibid., 121.

15 Abraham Lincoln, "Speech at Springfield, Ill.," June 26, 1857, Roy P. Basler, ed., *The Collected Works of Abraham Lincoln* (New Brunswick, N.J.: Rutgers University Press, 1953), II.406

16 *See* below, p. 17 for Zuckert's misreading of this passage.

17 *Collected Works of Abraham Lincoln*, II.266 (emphasis original).

18 Jaffa, *A New Birth of Freedom*, 336.

19 Ibid., 335.

20 Ibid.

21 Field-Marshal Viscount Wolseley, *The Story of a Soldier's Life* (Westminster: Archibald Constable and Company, Ltd., 1903) (2 vols.) II.102–103.

22 Jaffa, "Straussian Geography," in *Crisis of the Strauss Divided*, 1–13.

23 "Expediency and Morality in the Lincoln–Douglas Debates," was first published in *The Anchor Review* and given as a public lecture at St. John's College, Annapolis, Maryland, November 30, 1951.

24 Jaffa, "Straussian Geography," in *Crisis of the Strauss Divided*, 13.

25 Zuckert, "Jaffa's New Birth: Harry Jaffa at Ninety," in *Crisis*

of the Strauss Divided, 248.

26   Leo Strauss, *Natural Right and History*, 134–5.

27   Zuckert, "Jaffa's New Birth: Harry Jaffa at Ninety," in *Crisis of the Strauss Divided*, 250.

28   Michael P. Zuckert, *A Nation So Conceived: Abraham Lincoln and the Paradox of Democratic Sovereignty* (Lawrence, KS.: University Press of Kansas, 2023), 103.

29   Ibid. "self-ownership," of course, is the language of John Locke.

30   Ibid.

31   "Speech at Peoria, Ill.," Oct., 16, 1854, in *Collected Works of Abraham Lincoln* II.266 (emphasis original).

32   James Madison, "Sovereignty," in Gaillard Hunt, ed., *The Writings of James Madison* (New York: G.P. Putnam's Sons, 1908), 9:659. *See* Jaffa, *New Birth of Freedom*, 45–50; *see* also Jaffa "Equality, Liberty, Wisdom, Morality and Consent In the Idea of Political Freedom, in Erler and Masugi, eds., *The Rediscovery of America*, 44–45.

33   Michael P. Zuckert, "Self-Evident Truth and the Declaration of Independence," *The Review of Politics*, vol. 49, no. 3 (Summer 1987), 323, 328–9, 335.

34   Michael P. Zuckert, *The Natural Rights Republic: Studies in the Foundation of the American Political Tradition* (Notre Dame, In.: University of Notre Dame Press, 1996), 26,

35   *See* Jaffa's comments on the "Preface to the 7th Impression (1971)" of *Natural Right and History* in *Crisis of the Strauss Divided*, 91–2.

36   This axiom is convenient for explaining equality because it contains the words same (Τὰ τῷ αὐτῷ) and equal (ἴσα). This axiom is not exclusive to Euclid; it appeared before Euclid in Aristotle's *Topics*, VII, 1 (152 a1–33), although Aristotle does not call it an "axiom."

37 "Letter to Henry L. Pierce and Others," April 6, 1859, in *Collected Works of Abraham Lincoln*, III.375.

38 *See* Lincoln, "Autobiography Written for John L. Scripps," written about June 1860, in *Collected Works of Abraham Lincoln*, IV.62.

39 *See* Eva Brann, "A Reading of the Gettysburg Address," in Leo Paul S. de Alvarez, ed., *Abraham Lincoln, the Gettysburg Address, and American Constitutionalism* (Dallas, Tx.: University of Dallas Press, 1976), 14–53; Diana Schaub, *His Greatest Speeches: How Lincoln Moved the Nation* (New York, N.Y.: St Martin's Press, 2021), 59–108; John Channing Briggs, *Lincoln's Speeches Reconsidered* (Baltimore, Md.: Johns University Press, 2005), 303–315, especially, 308, 311.

40 "Speech at Peoria," in *Collected Works*, II.249.

41 *See* Harry Jaffa, *Crisis of the House Divided* (Garden City, N.Y.: Doubleday & Co., 1959), 211.

42 Thomas Jefferson, "Letter to Roger C. Weightman," June 24, 1826, in *Jefferson: Papers*, 1517. This was the last letter that Jefferson ever wrote; it was to decline an invitation to attend a celebration for the fiftieth anniversary of the Declaration of Independence. Jefferson died on July 4, 1826, the fiftieth anniversary, the same day as John Adams, his principal co-author. *See* Abraham Lincoln, "Response to a Serenade," July 7, 1863, in *Collected Works of Abraham Lincoln*, VI.319–20. "The two most distinguished men in the framing and support of the Declaration were Thomas Jefferson and John Adams—the one having penned it and the other sustained it the most forcibly in debate. . . . Precisely fifty years after they put their hands to the paper it pleased Almighty God to take both from the stage of action. This was indeed an extraordinary and remarkable event in our history."

43   Thomas Jefferson, "Letter to Henri Gregoire, February 25, 1809, in Merrill Peterson, ed., *Jefferson: Writings* (New York: Library of America, 1984), 1202.

44   *Collected Works of Abraham Lincoln*, II.278.

45   Ibid., III.315.

46   *A New Birth of Freedom*, 127.

47   *See* also, "Straussian Geography," in *Crisis of the Strauss Divided*, 32–33.

48   *Collected Works of Abraham Lincoln*, II.255 (italics original).

49   See Edward Erler, *Property and the Pursuit of Happiness: Locke, the Declaration of Independence, Madison, and the Challenge of the Administrative State* (Lanham, Md.: Rowman and Littlefield, 2019), Ch. 2.

50   *Collected Works of Abraham Lincoln*, IV.17.

51   Ibid., 19–20 (emphasis original).

52   Leo Strauss, "On Classical Political Philosophy," in *What is Political? And Other Studies* (New York: Free Press, 1959), 86.

53   Thomas Jefferson, "Letter to John Adams," October 28, 1813, in Merrill Peterson, ed., *Jefferson: Writings*, 1306.

54   Jaffa, "A Reply to Michael Zuckert's 'Jaffa's New Birth: Harry Jaffa at Ninety'," in *Crisis of the Strauss Divided*, 262.

55   Ibid., 263. *See* Strauss, "Restatement on Xenophon's *Hiero*" in *What is Political Philosophy?*, 113, 132.

56   Ibid., 265.

57   Steven B. Smith, *Reading Leo Strauss: Politics, Philosophy, Judaism* (Chicago: University of Chicago Press, 2006), 170.

58   Ibid., 172–3.

59   Leo Strauss, *Natural Right and History*, 165.

60   Smith, *Reading Leo Strauss*, 173.

61   Ibid.

62   Catherine and Michael Zuckert, *The Truth About Leo*

Strauss: Political Philosophy and American Democracy (Chicago: University of Chicago Press, 2006), 249.

63 Ibid. Both of these footnotes are to Jaffa rather than Strauss.

64 Ibid., 136–37.

65 Harry Jaffa wrote in *A New Birth of Freedom* (at 124) that "Sometimes the best argument is the least persuasive, and the most persuasive argument is far from being the best. That those who dissemble often do so in the cause of injustice does not mean that those who dissemble may not do so in the interest of justice."

66 Leo Strauss, *On Tyranny: An Interpretation of Xenophon's Hiero* (Glencoe, Il.: The Free Press, 1948), 1.

67 Leo Strauss, *The City and Man* (Chicago: Rand McNally, 1964), 89; *see Natural Right and History*, 227.

68 Ibid., 11.

69 Harry Jaffa, "Straussian Geography," in *Crisis of the Strauss Divided*, 30. The reference to "modernity is bad and that America is modern" is from Catherine and Michael Zuckert, *The Truth About Leo Strauss*, 21.

70 Catherine and Michael Zuckert write that "[t]he first and perhaps chief consequence of Strauss's recovery of the ancients was therefore a reconceiving of the entire philosophic tradition. Not only did he come to understand the classics differently from the way they had been understood, but he also radicalized a commonplace distinction between ancients and moderns. With the emergence of modern philosophy, a break of such magnitude that all that came after was simply a working out of the implications of that break. In the Straussian frame, the difference between ancients and moderns became decisive."

71 Jaffa, "A Reply to Michael Zuckert's 'Jaffa's *New Birth*: Harry

Jaffa at Ninety'," in *Crisis of the Strauss Divided*, 266, 267.

72   Ibid., 268.

73   Ibid. The same argument is made in *New Birth*": "In the Virginia and Massachusetts Bills of Rights, as in the Declaration, safety is the first of the ends or purposes of political life, but happiness is the end for which life, liberty, and property are wanted. Liberty and property come to sight as means to the preservation of life, but their enduring worth is in the service, not of mere life, but for the good or happy life. The natural wants or rights of man from which society springs are not random but ordered. And it is the natural order of these wants, directed toward their corresponding natural ends, that constitutes the architectonic principles of society arising out of compact, properly understood." 50.

Chapter Two

1   Harry V. Jaffa, *A New Birth of Freedom: Abraham Lincoln and the Coming of the Civil War* (Lanham, Md.: Rowman and Littlefield, 2000), 28, 30.

2   Merrill D. Peterson, ed. *Jefferson: Writings* (New York: Library of America, 1984), 479.

3   Alexander Hamilton, James Madison, and John Jay, *The Federalist Papers*, introduction and notes by Charles R. Kesler, ed. Clinton Rossiter (New York: Signet Classics, 1999), 22:148 (All emphasis original) (further references in the text by paper number and page). Professor Bradford Collins, Department of Political Science, The Citadel, pointed out the importance of Hamilton's argument.

4   *A New Birth of Freedom*, 59–60.

5   *A New Birth of Freedom*, 34.

6   Ibid., 278.

7   Thomas Jefferson, "Letter to Edward Carrington," Aug. 4,

1787, in Adrienne Koch and William Peden, eds., *The Life and Selected Writings of Thomas Jefferson* (New York: Modern Library, 1945), 427.

8   James Madison is justly famous for the speech he delivered before the House of Representatives on June 8, 1789, introducing the Bill of Rights. Madison suggested "there be prefixed to the constitution a declaration." He then proposed: "that all power is originally vested in, and consequently derived from, the people;" "that Government is instituted and ought to be exercised for the benefit of the people; which consists in the enjoyment of life and liberty, with the right of acquiring and using property, and generally of pursuing and obtaining happiness and safety;" "that the people have an indubitable, unalienable, and indefeasible right to reform or change their Government, whenever it be found adverse or inadequate to the purposes of its institution." ("Debates and Proceedings in the Congress of the United States," Gales & Seaton, eds., 451). The language that Madison desired to add the Constitution as a "declaration," reminds us of nothing so much as the Declaration of Independence, especially its invocation, in its last "declaration," of the right to revolution. It is odd, not to say almost incomprehensible, that the organic law of the nation would mention the natural right of revolution. At best, it is superfluous; at worst, it would seem dangerous (see Madison's criticism of Jefferson in *Federalist* 48:307–8). The people are never mentioned in this proposed constitutional "declaration," but the "people" are mentioned as ultimate sovereign in the Tenth Amendment—also Madison's handiwork but added after his suggestions for "declarations" as preambles had been rejected by the House! *See* Gales & Seaton, 745–7. *See* Robert A. Goldwin, *From Parchment to Power: How*

James Madison Used the Bill of Rights to Save the Constitution (Washington, D.C.: AEI Press, 1997), 86–89; Edward Erler, "James Madison and the Framing of the Bill of Rights: Reality and Rhetoric in the New Constitutionalism," 9 *Political Communication* 213–229 (1992).

9   Harry V. Jaffa, *A New Birth of Freedom*, 8. The point made here by Jaffa about elections and the right of revolution as it pertains to the protection of minority rights is a different argument and not, I believe, in tension with the one made earlier about the right of revolution also being a ground for deliberation.

10   James Madison, "Sovereignty," in Gaillard Hunt, ed., *The Writings of James Madison* (New York, N.Y.: G.P. Putnam's Sons, 1908), 9:570.

11   Ibid.

12   Ibid., 570–71 ("*rightfully*" emphasized in original).

13   *A New Birth of Freedom*, 118.

14   *See* Edward J. Erler, *Property and the Pursuit of Happiness* (Lanham, Md.: Rowman and Littlefield, 2019), 73–82.

15   Harry V. Jaffa, *A New of Freedom*, 6–7.

16   Ibid., 9.

17   *A New Birth of Freedom*, 260. *See* 12: "[F]or Jefferson, no less than for Aristotle, what men seek by nature is not the ancestral but the good." Also 207: The founders "did not simply preserve the inheritance from their fathers. On the contrary, as Aristotle would say, they chose the good over the ancestral."

18   *See* Ch. 5, *infra*, pp. 12 ff.

19   *A New Birth of Freedom*, 263.

20   Ibid., 263–4.

21   *See* Chapter five, *infra*, pp. 42–5 and footnote 62 discussing Randy E. Barnett and Evan D. Bernick, *The Original*

Endnotes

Meaning of the 14th Amendment: Its Letter & Spirit.

22 *Dred Scott v. Sandford*, 60 U.S. 393 (19 How. 393) (1857), 423.

23 *Congressional Globe*, 39th Cong., 1st Sess., 1088 (1866) (Rep. Bingham, Republican, Ohio).

24 *Congressional Globe*, 42nd Cong., 1st Sess. (March 31, 1871), Appendix, 83 (Rep. Bingham, Republican, Ohio).

25 *A New Birth of Freedom*, 267.

26 Kurt T. Lash, *The Fourteenth Amendment and the Privileges and Immunities of American Citizenship* (New York, N.Y.: Cambridge University Press, 2014), 85–93. *See* Edward Erler, *Property and the Pursuit of Happiness*, 177–79.

27 *A New Birth of Freedom*, 267.

28 *A New Birth of Freedom*, 271,

29 Ibid.

30 Ibid., 272 (emphasis original).

31 Ibid., 273.

32 Ibid., 274.

33 Ibid., 276.

34 *Dred Scott v. Sandford*, at 451.

35 *A New Birth of Freedom*, 280.

36 "Sovereignty," 569.

37 Ibid., 571.

38 *A New Birth of Freedom*, 285.

39 *A New Birth of Freedom*, 341–42.

40 Ibid., 342–43.

41 Ibid., 344–45.

42 Ibid., 347.

43 *A New Birth of Freedom*, 349.

44 Ibid.

45 Ibid., 351–352.

46 Ibid., 352.

47 Ibid., 352. *See* chapter one, pp. 8–10. Jaffa argues there that

that Jefferson's "Virginia Statute for Religious Freedom" and Madison's "Memorial and Remonstrance" "are the greatest documents of human freedom in all human history."

48   Ibid., 353.

49   Ibid. Jaffa quotes from, "Speech at Lewistown, Illinois," August 17 1858, *Collected Works of Abraham Lincoln*, II.546–47. I have shortened the quotation presented by Jaffa. The editor of Lincoln's *Collected Works* suggests there may be some questions about the authenticity of the exact language of the speech.

50   This phrase is from a fragment of unknown origin published in the *Collected Works* as "Definition of Democracy," II.532.

51   *A New Birth of Freedom*, 353.

Chapter Three

1   Harry V. Jaffa, *Crisis of the House Divided: An Interpretation of the Lincoln–Douglas Debates* (Garden City, N.Y.: Doublday & Co., 1959), 205.

2   "Lyceum Address," in Roy P. Basler, ed., *The Collected Works of Abraham Lincoln* (New Brunswick, N.J.: Rutgers University Press, 1954), I.111 (emphasis original).

3   Ibid., I.112 (emphasis original). Lincoln's odd use of "breathed" here probably reflects his reading of Ezekiel 34. *See* below note 36.

4   Ibid., I.114 (emphasis original).

5   Jaffa, *Crisis of the House Divided*, 211

6   Ibid., 218.

7   Ibid.

8   Charles R. Kesler, "A New Birth of Freedom," in Kenneth L. Deutsch and John Murley, eds., *Leo Strauss, the Straussians, and the American Regime* (Lanham, Md.: Rowman &

Littlefield, 1999), 270–71.

9   *A New Birth of Freedom*, xii.

10   *Crisis of the House Divided*, 306.

11   Leo Strauss, "What is Liberal Education," in *Liberalism Ancient and Modern* (New York, N.Y.: Basic Books, Inc., 1968), 4.

12   "Liberal Education and Responsibility," in Ibid., 24.

13   "Restatement on Xenophon's *Hiero*," in *What is Political Philosophy? and Other Essays* (New York, N.Y.: The Free Press, 1959), 113. This essay was first published in 1954 in French.

14   Thomas Jefferson, "Autobiography," in Merrill D. Peterson, ed., *Thomas Jefferson: Writings* (New York, N.Y.: Library of America, 1984), 32.

15   "Liberal Education and Responsibility," 21.

16   *See* Chapter 1, p. 2.

17   *Laws* 757 d.

18   In "What is Political Philosophy?", delivered first as lectures at Hebrew University, Jerusalem in December 1954 and January 1955 and first published in Hebrew in 1955. The first publication of the two lectures in English was as the title essay in *What is Political Philosophy? and Other Essays* published in 1959. Strauss contends (p. 32) that the Athenian Stranger was in fact Socrates. He points out that the *Apology of Socrates* is the only dialogue that ends with the word "God," and the *Laws* is the only dialogue that begins with the word "God." This fact suggests not only a connection between the two dialogues but the order in which they should be read. As a parenthetical note, Strauss remarks that "[w]hen Aristotle speaks about Plato's *Laws*, he takes it for granted that the chief character of the *Laws* is Socrates" (p. 33). Strauss exaggerates slightly here because Aristotle never names Socrates, referring to "he," "he said,"

"it is said," or "in the *Laws*." *See The Politics of Aristotle*, translated with Introduction, Analysis, and Notes, by Peter L. Philips-Simpson (Chapel Hill, N.C.: University of North Carolina Press, 1997), 45, note 34. Simpson admits that these reference "would seem to be Socrates." "We are entitled to infer," Strauss writes, "that if Socrates had fled, he would gone to Crete. The *Laws* tells us what he would have done in Crete after his arrival: he would have brought the blessings of Athens, Athenian laws, Athenian institutions, banquets, and philosophy to Crete." Socrates, in short, would have become the founder of a new regime, a philosophic founder! Instead, "Socrates chose to die in Athens. Socrates preferred to sacrifice his life in order to preserve philosophy in Athens rather than to preserve his life in order introduce philosophy into Crete." Strauss concludes that Socrates' "choice was a political choice of the highest order. It did not consist in the simple subsumption of his case under a simple, universal, and unalterable rule." In other words, it was a prudent choice. As Strauss suggests, the choice might have been different had Socrates been 40 instead of 70 at the time of the choice! A more elaborate (and serious) defense of this thesis is presented by Strauss in *The Argument and the Action of Plato's Laws* (Chicago: University of Chicago Press, 1972), 2.

19   "Eulogy on Henry Clay," *Collected Works of Abraham Lincoln*, I:122; Michael P. Zuckert, *A Nation So Conceived: Abraham Lincoln and the Paradox of Democratic Sovereignty* (Lawrence, Ks.: University Press of Kansas, 2023), 71.

20   Zuckert, *A Nation So Conceived*, 71–72; John Channing Briggs, *Lincoln's Speeches Reconsidered* (Baltimore, Md.: The Johns Hopkins University Press, 2005), 117.

21   Only a Shakespeare scholar would use such a word. See

Antony and Cleopatra, IV.xii.22 (Antony).

22 Briggs, *Lincoln's Speeches Reconsidered*, 132.

23 "Letter to George Robertson," August 15, 1855, in *Collected Works of Abraham Lincoln*, II.318 (emphasis original).

24 *See* above chapter one, footnote 3.

25 "Fragment: Last Speech of the Campaign at Springfield, Illinois," October 30, 1858, *Collected Works of Abraham Lincoln*, III.334 (emphasis original).

26 Matthew Holbreich and Danilo Petranovich, "In the Valley of the Dry Bones: Lincoln's Biblical Oratory and the Coming of the Civil War," *History of Political Thought*, vol. xxxv, no. 1 (Spring, 2014), 140.

27 *Collected Works of Abraham Lincoln*, II.461.

28 Ibid., 461–2,

29 Holbreich and Petrovich, 140–142.

30 *A New Birth of Freedom*, 324,

31 "A House Divided," Speech at Springfield, Illinois, June 16, 1858, in *Collected Works of Abraham Lincoln*, II.467 (all emphasis original).

32 Holbreich and Petranovich, 142.

33 *Ecclesiasties*, 9:4.

34 Ibid., 9:14–16.

35 Holbreich and Petranovich, 142.

36 "A House Divided," in *Collected Works of Abraham Lincoln*, II.468 (all emphasis original).

37 Ezekiel, 37:1–10.

38 Holbreich and Petranovich, 132.

39 Ibid., 133; 123, 129.

40 Ibid., 143.

41 Letter to John L. Scripps, June 23, 1858, *Collected Works of Abraham Lincoln*, II.470.

42 Holbreich and Petranovich, 143.

43   *Crisis of the House Divided*, 278.

44   Ibid., 294.

45   *Collected Works of Abraham Lincoln*, II.465–66.

46   *Congressional Globe*, 34th Cong., 1st Sess. 797, 1371–72 (1856);
       See David M. Potter, *The Impending Crisis, 1848–1861* (New
       York: Harper and Row, 1976), 74, 116, 161, 271, 276, 285, 292,
       294, 403, 410.

47   *A Compilation of the Messages and Papers of the Presidents*,
       James D. Richardson, ed. (Washington, D.C.: Bureau of
       National Literature and Art, 1905), 5:348.

48   Ibid., V:431.

49   Potter, 287, note 36. A full account of the correspondence
       between President Buchanan and Justices Catron and Grier
       is in Paul Finkelman, "James Buchanan, Dred Scott, and
       the Whisper of Conspiracy," in John W. Quist and Michael
       J. Birkner, eds., *James Buchanan and the Coming of the Civil
       War* (Gainesville, Fl.: University of Florida Press, 2013),
       39–41. Buchanan lobbied members of the Court in several
       exchanges to declare the Missouri Compromise unconsti-
       tutional. Finkelman concludes that "[t]his correspondence
       shows that Lincoln's instincts were right. Buchanan had
       conspired directly with two members of the Court, and
       indirectly (through Grier) with Taney and Justice Wayne.
       Lincoln, Seward, and other Republicans could not name all
       the conspirators, but the improper communications were
       there, and so was the plan, by at least four members for the
       Court and the president-elect, to make sure a decision came
       out as Buchanan and Taney wanted. The conspiracy was
       both less elaborate than Lincoln believed, because Douglas
       was clearly not involved, but also more elaborate, because it
       involved at least four justices. Buchanan had worked with,
       communicated with, and indeed conspired with members

of the Supreme Court to lay the groundwork for *Dred Scott*" (at 40–41). Finkelman here agrees with Lincoln that, with the exception of Douglas, this amounts to a "conspiracy." Three years later, however, Finkelman says that it amounts only to a "collusion." *See* below footnote 62. One wonders whether Douglas' endorsement of the *Dred Scott* decision after it was announced should be counted as evidence that he was part of the conspiracy as Lincoln believed.

50   *Dred Scott v. Sandford*, 60 U.S. (19 How.), 393, 451, 407 (1857).

51   Ibid., 407, 410.

52   Ibid., 574–76.

53   Paul Finkelman, *An Imperfect Union: Slavery, Federalism, and Comity* (Chapel Hill, N.C.: University of North Carolina Press, 1981), 326.

54   *Dred Scott*, 468 (Nelson, J., concurring).

55   *Collected Works of Abraham Lincoln*, III.548. *See* Finkelman, 319.

56   *Lemmon v. The People of New York*, 20 N.Y. 562, 609, 611 (1860).

57   Finkelman, *An Imperfect Union*, 326.

58   *See* Paul Finkelman, *Dred Scott v. Sandford: A Brief History with Documents*, 2nd ed. (Boston, MA: Bedford/St. Martin's, 2017), 43.

59   "Speech of Stephen Douglas," Chicago, July 9, in *The Lincoln–Douglas Debates of 1858*, Robert W. Johannsen, ed. (New York: Oxford University Press, 1965), 31; *See Collected Works of Abraham Lincoln*, III.9, 54, 242, 267, 287.

60   *Collected Works of Abraham Lincoln*, III.143.

61   Ibid., 255.

62   *In re Archy*, 9 Cal. 147, 162 (1858) (emphasis original). *See* William E. Franklin, "The Archy Case: The California

Supreme Court Refuses to Free a Slave," *Pacific Historical Review*, vol. 32 (1963), 137–154.

63 *See* Paul Finkelman, *Dred Scott v. Sandford: A Brief History*, 41. "There may not have been an ongoing conspiracy, but collusion abounded. The Court and the president-elect worked closely to get the decision Buchanan and Taney wanted and to urge the nation to accept it." The line Finkelman draws between collusion and conspiracy is a very fine one! Buchanan and Taney undoubtedly had a common understanding! In any case, serious questions about the separation of powers arise, even if the legislative and executive branches agreed to allow the judiciary to decide.

64 Jaffa, *Crisis of the House Divided*, 285–86.

65 Ibid., 286.

66 *Collected Works of Abraham Lincoln*, IV.16–17.

67 "Speech at Springfield, Illinois," June 26, 1857, in *Collected Works of Abraham Lincoln*, II.405.

68 Ibid., II.409.

69 Ibid.

70 This is an example of Lincoln appealing to white prejudice in a good cause. As Jaffa remarked in *A New Birth of Freedom*, (124) it does not "mean that to be sincere, one must always put forward the best or truest argument in support of one's cause. Sometimes the best argument is the least persuasive, and the most persuasive argument is far from being the best. That those who dissemble often do so in the cause of injustice does not mean that those who dissemble may not do so in the interest of justice."

71 Ibid. Lincoln revealed his ultimate opposition to colonization in his Second Annual Message delivered to Congress on December 1, 1862, where he said "there is an objection urged against free colored persons remaining in the country,

which is largely imaginary if not sometimes malicious." For a fuller account *see* Erler, "The Fourteenth Amendment and the Completion of the Constitution: Abraham Lincoln and Reconstruction," in William B. Allen, ed., *The State of Black America: Progress, Pitfalls, and The Promise of the Republic* (New York, N.Y.: Encounter Books, 2022), 106, 105–110.

72 Ibid.

73 Diana Schaub, *His Greatest Speeches: How Lincoln Moved the Nation* (New York, N.Y.: St. Martin's Press, 2021), 103–106. For the analysis of Holbreich and Petranovich, *see* above pp. 15–21.

74 *See* chapter one, pp. 12–13.

Chapter Four

1 Harry Jaffa, "The Speech that Changed the World," *Interpretation: A Journal of Political Philosophy*, vol. 24, no. 2 (Spring, 1997), 363.

2 Ibid. (emphasis original).

3 George Anastaplo, *Abraham Lincoln: A Constitutional Biography* (Lanham, Md.: Rowman and Littlefield, 1999), 232.

4 *See* Harry Jaffa, *A New Birth of Freedom: Abraham Lincoln and the Coming of the Civil War* (Lanham, Md., Rowman and Littlefield, 2000), 78.

5 Anastaplo, *Abraham Lincoln*, 232.

6 Eva Brann, "A Reading of the Gettysburg Address," in Leo Paul S. de Alvarez, ed., *Abraham Lincoln: The Gettysburg Address and American Constitutionalism* (Dallas, TX.: University of Dallas Press, 1976), 21; Diana Schaub, *His Greatest Speeches: How Lincoln Moved the Nation* (New York, N.Y.: St. Martin's, 2021), 70.

7 Anastaplo, *Abraham Lincoln*, 233.

8 Lincoln, "Peoria Speech," Oct. 16, 1854, in Roy P. Basler, ed.,

The Collected Works of Abraham Lincoln (New Brunswick,
N.J.: 1953), II.266 (Consent of the governed "is the leading
principle—the sheet anchor of American Republicanism.")
See Jefferson, "First Inaugural," in Merrill D. Peterson,
ed., *Thomas Jefferson: Writings* (New York, N.Y.: Library
of America, 1984), 494, also uses "sheet anchor" in the
same sense.

9   Schaub, *His Greatest Speeches*, 68–69. *See* Eva Brann, "A
Reading of the Gettysburg Address," 22–23.

10   Ibid., 69. A simpler explanation would be that the number
87 in "eighty-seven years ago" would draw the attention of
the audience to the date of the Constitutional Convention
and the erroneous impression that Lincoln was pointing
to the Constitution rather than the Declaration of Independence as the true founding document. But this simple
explanation would deprive Professors Schaub and Jaffa (discussed in the next paragraph) of their poetic interpretations
which I find have great merit.

11   *Crisis of the House Divided: An Interpretation of the Lincoln–
Douglas Debates* (Garden City, N.Y., 1959: Doubleday and
Company), 330, 228. *See* Appendix.

12   Ibid., 228.

13   "Autobiography Written for John L. Scripps," in *Collected
Works of Abraham Lincoln*, IV.62. (An editorial note indi-
cates that "Lincoln prepared this sketch for the guidance
of John L. Scripps, who was writing a campaign biography
to be published by the Chicago *Press and Tribune*. Scripps'
Life was also issued by Horace Greeley as *Tribune Tracts
No. 6*. *See* also Eva Brann, "A Reading of the Gettysburg
Address," 25.

14   *Crisis of the House Divided*, 230.

15   *See*, e.g., Erler, *Property and the Pursuit of Happiness*

(Lanham, Md.: Rowman and Littlefield, 2019), 54–60.

16   *Crisis of the House Divided*, 330–331.

17   *Collected Works of Abraham Lincoln*, II.275 (emphasis original).

18   Ibid.

19   *Collected Works of Abraham Lincoln*, II.255 (emphasis original).

20   *Collected Works of Abraham Lincoln*, II.398. This speech was previously addressed in Chapter one, at 9–11.

21   "Speech at Springfield, Illinois," June 26, 1857, *Collected Works*: II.405–406 (emphasis original).

22   Ibid.

23   *A New Birth of Freedom*, 299; *see* 395, 421 "Lincoln is constantly refining and perfecting the articulation if that 'central idea' *that will take its final form at Gettysburg.* The proposition that all men are created equal can no more distinguish the color of those to whom it refers than can the Golden Rule propounded by Jesus. It is 'the condition of men,' not of one class only or one race only, that is to be ameliorated" (emphasis added),

24   *Crisis of the Strauss Divided*, 228.

25   See Madison's speech at the Virginia Ratifying Convention, June 17, 1788, in Robert A. Rutland, et al., eds., *The Papers of James Madison* (Chicago: University of Chicago Press, 1962), 11:150–151.

26   See e.g., James Wilson's speech at the Pennsylvania Ratifying Convention, December 4, 1787, in John McMaster and Frederick Stone, eds., *Pennsylvania and the Federal Constitution 1787–1788* (Indianapolis: Liberty Fund, 2011 [first published in 1888]), 311–312.

27   *Collected Works of Abraham Lincoln*, II:461, 492, 498, 501, 514, 520–21; 3:18, 78, 87, 92–3, 117, 180–81, 254–55, 276,

307, 312–13, 333,404, 406–7, 439, 483, 488, 489, 498, 535, 537–38, 550, 551, 553; 4:17–18, 21–22.

28 *See A New Birth of Freedom*, 297: "Taney's pseudo-Kantian attempt to infer the 'true' meaning of the Declaration from the failure of the Founders to abolish slavery would have been merely ludicrous had it not been welcomed as supplying the constitutional justification for everything the proslavery South was demanding and, ultimately, for rejecting the results of the 1860 presidential election. . . . The Declaration itself endorses the dictates of prudence, thereby endorsing a prudential morality that is the very antithesis of Kant's categorical imperative." *See* also 292–3, 301–302, 311.

29 "Speech at Chicago, Ill.," July 10, 1858, *Collected Works of Abraham Lincoln*, II.499. This speech was a reply to a speech given by Douglas at the same location the day before.

30 *Collected Works of Abraham Lincoln*, II.375.

31 Eva Brann, "Á Reading of the Gettysburg Address," 25.

32 Ibid.

33 "Speech at Peoria, Illinois," Oct. 16, 1854, *Collected Works of Abraham Lincoln*, II.249.

34 *See* Chapter One, pp. 20–24.

35 "Letter to Henry L. Pierce and Others," April 6, 1859, in *Collected Works of Abraham Lincoln*, III.376.

36 *See* Chapter One, 21–23.

37 An intelligent discussion of "conceived in Liberty" is to be found in Schaub, *His Greatest Speeches: How Lincoln Moved the Nation*, 75–78. She calls it "this language of sexual congress," and notes that "'to conceive' can denote either a physical or mental phenomenon: becoming pregnant or taking a notion into the mind. Before the nation could be brought forth into practical realization, it had to be thought of or imagined. When arose the concept? According to

Lincoln, it originated 'in Liberty.' . . . Why does Lincoln in-
carnate liberty in this way. . .?" That is indeed the question!

38   *The Collected Works of Abraham Lincoln*, IV.438.

39   Ibid., 439.

40   Leo Strauss, *Natural Right and History* (Chicago: University
of Chicago Press, 1953), 2.

41   *Crisis of the Strauss Divided*, 14. I argued in a previous
chapter, against the weight of scholarly opinion, that it was
the clearly avowed purpose of the thirty ninth congress to
restore the principles of the Declaration of Independence
in their understanding of the 14th Amendment. This would
bring the Constitution into formal harmony with the original intentions of the founders.

42   "Annual Message to Congress," December 1, 1862, in *Collected Works of Abraham Lincoln*, V.537 (emphasis original).

43   Ibid., V.530.

44   Carl L. Becker, *The Declaration of Independence: A Study in
the History of Political Ideas* (New York, N.Y.: Vintage Books,
1942), 277 [first published in 1922].

45   *A New Birth of Freedom*, 75.

46   Becker, *The Declaration of Independence*, 265–66.

47   Jaffa, *A New Birth of Freedom*, 84–5.

48   See above fn. 28.

Chapter Five

1   Edward J. Erler, "*Marbury v. Madison* and the Progressive
Transformation of Judicial Power," in John Marini and Ken
Masugi, eds., *The Progressive Revolution in Politics and Politi-
cal Science: Transforming the American Regime* (Lanham,
M.D.: Rowman and Littlefield, 2015), 216, note 111.

2   Michael Burlingame, *Abraham Lincoln: A Life* (Baltimore,
M.D.: Johns Hopkins University Press, 2008), 2:47. It is not

known if Lincoln ever read *David Copperfield*, although it is safe to assume he must have read some Dickens.

3   Diana Schaub, *His Greatest Speeches: How Lincoln Moved the Nation* (New York, N.Y.: St. Martin's Press, 2021), 114. *See* Ronald C. White, Jr., *Lincoln's Greatest Speech: The Second Inaugural* (New York: N.Y.: Simon and Schuster Paperbacks, 2002, 76.

4   Harry V. Jaffa, *A New Birth of Freedom: Abraham Lincoln and the Coming of the Civil War* (Lanham, M.D.: Rowman and Littlefield, 2000), 94.

5   Ibid., 128.

6   *See* Schaub, *His Greatest Speeches*, 158. Schaub writes that "Jefferson had tried to frighten his fellow slaveholders into considering gradual emancipation by reminding them of God's sympathies." *See* Jaffa, *Crisis of the Strauss Divided: Essays on Leo Strauss and Straussianism, East and West* (Lanham, M.D.: Rowman and Littlefield, 2012), 265.

7   Thomas Jefferson, *Jefferson: Writings*, Merrill D. Peterson, ed. (New York, N.Y.: Library of America, 1984), 289 (Query XVIII).

8   Ibid.

9   *Collected Works of Abraham Lincoln*, Roy P. Basler, ed. (New Brunswick, N.J.: Rutgers University Press, 1953), IV.268–69 (emphasis original).

10 Ibid., IV.268.

11 Schaub, *His Greatest Speeches*, 144.

12 Ibid.

13 *Collected Works of Abraham Lincoln*, IV.403–04.

14 Jaffa, *A New Birth of Freedom*, 153.

15 Ibid., 155. *See*, 352 for Jaffa's revealing commentary on paragraph thirty-three of Lincoln's First Inaugural, the first of his "fitting and proper" speeches.

16 Schaub, *His Greatest Speeches*, 149.

17 Schaub, *His Greatest Speeches*, 156.

18 The forgoing is based on Edward Erler, "The Fourteenth Amendment and the Completion of the Constitution: Abraham Lincoln and Reconstruction," in William B. Allen, ed., *The State of Black America: Progress, Pitfalls, and the Promise of the Republic* (New York, N.Y.: Encounter Books, 2022), 69–126.

Appendix

1 "Letter to James H. Hackett," August 17, 1863, in Roy P. Basler, ed., *The Collected Works of Abraham Lincoln* (Rutgers, N.J.: Rutgers University Press, 1953), VI.392.

2 Harry V. Jaffa, *A New Birth of Freedom: Abraham Lincoln and the Coming of the Civil War* (Lanham, MD.: Rowman and Littlefield, 2000), 128.

3 "Speech at Peoria, Illinois," in *The Collected Works of Abraham Lincoln*, II.276 (emphasis original).

4 Harry Jaffa cites Hamlet III.l.76–82 to the same purpose. Jaffa prefaces this citation with these remarks from Lincoln's First Inaugural: Lincoln will repeat, Jaffa says, "what he said earlier about the Declaration of Independence. That will reappear after Fort Sumter, in his July 4 message to Congress and again, *most concisely, in the Gettysburg Address.* Implicit in everything he says, however, is the thesis that the benefits of free society cannot be long enjoyed by those who would arbitrarily deny them to others. . . . Hence the underlying question remains: Can those for whom slavery is a 'positive good' or those who are indifferent to slavery love the Union as do those for whom the Union is the practical implementation of the principles of human freedom embodied in the Declaration?" (emphasis

added). Jaffa's commentary on Hamlet's soliloquy is that "[u]nlike Hamlet, the secessionists are flying toward death, not away from it. They are flying not only toward civil war but also toward the reversal of those hopes of popular government that accompanied the Founding." That is the clear an unequivocal connection to the Gettysburg Address. Harry Jaffa, *A New Birth of Freedom*, 274.

5   Marquis de Chambrun, "Personal Recollections of Mr. Lincoln," *Scribner's Magazine*, 13 (1893), 35 (all emphasis original); *See* David Donald, *Lincoln* (London: Johnathan Cape, 1995), 580.

6   "Speech at Peoria, Illinois," October 16, 1854, in ibid., II.270 (emphasis original). The timing of the remark in Hamlet is crucial and will be noted in due course.

1   Harry V. Jaffa, "The Unity of Tragedy, Comedy, and History: An Interpretation of the Shakespearean Universe," in John Alvis and Thomas G. West, eds., *Shakespeare as Political Thinker* (Durham, N.C.: Carolina Academic Press, 1981), 277–303.

2   *See* Harry V. Jaffa, "Equality, Liberty, Wisdom, Morality, and Consent in the Idea of Political Freedom," in Edward J. Erler and Ken Masugi, eds., *The Rediscovery of America: Essays by Harry V. Jaffa on the New Birth of Politics* (Lanham, Md.: Rowman and Littlefield, 2012), 11–46; *especially* appendix, 40–45. Originally published in *Interpretation: A Journal of Political Philosophy*, vol. 15, no. 1 (Jan. 1987).

3   "Thomas Aquinas Meets Thomas Jefferson," in Erler and Masugi, eds., *The Rediscovery of America*, 265–274. Originally published in *Interpretation: A Journal of Political Philosophy*, vol. 33, no. 2 (Spring, 2006).

4   "New Introduction" to the Claremont Institute edition of *Thomism and Aristotelianism*, forthcoming.

5   Harry V. Jaffa, *Crisis of the Strauss Divided*, 225–26. Jaffa
     showed that he could select whimsical titles for books,
     "Crisis of the Strauss Divided" being a frivolous play on
     "Crisis of the House Divided" suggested by one of his
     former students, herself a noted political philosopher. Jaffa
     also "selected" chapter 17 for the placement of his essay
     "Too Good to be True?" in which he demonstrated that
     Aquinas, Jefferson, Washington, and Lincoln engaged in
     non-historicist thought. The number 17 for those who fol-
     low such things was the "classical" number for philosophy.
     Jaffa was whimsical and serious. Although the title of the
     chapter is not enclosed in quotation marks, I am almost
     certain it is taken from a phrase used by Professor Charles
     R. Kesler in his essay, "A New Birth of Freedom: Harry V.
     Jaffa and the Study of America," in Kenneth L. Deutsch and
     John A. Murley, eds., *Leo Strauss, the Straussians, and the
     American Regime* (Lanham, Md.: Rowman and Littlefield,
     1999), 273. Commenting on Jaffa's account of the Lyceum
     Speech regarding Lincoln's presentation of the men of su-
     perior talents and abilities (those who belong to the "family
     of the lion or the tribe of the eagle") Kesler says "[e]xtreme
     human inequality and fundamental human equality were
     both true. This result may itself seem either too good to be
     true—a '*political truth*' is hardly the whole truth—or too
     true to be good, insofar as it appears to sideline all human
     virtue that fell short of the godlike. But Jaffa's point was
     that it was impossible to do justice to human equality and
     to human inequality at the same time in politics" (emphasis
     original). Jaffa was determined to refute Kesler's point that
     "it was impossible to do justice to human equality and to
     human inequality at the same time in politics." I believe
     Jaffa's account of Lincoln's Aristotelian statesmanship

succeeded in doing so.

6   Jaffa, *Crisis of the Strauss Divided*, 21.

7   *See* footnote 2 above.

8   Jaffa, "Aristotle and Locke in the American Founding,"
     in Erler and Masugi, eds., *The Rediscovery of America*, 6
     (reprinted from the *Claremont Review of Books*, vol. 1, no. 2
     (Winter, 2001).

INDEX

230

Clause as part of debate over, 70–71; shared injustice of, 163; state control over, 73; text of House Divided Speech expressing opinion about, 70

Smith, Steven B., 39

social compact: Madison on, 63–65; republican government and, 32; Zuckert and, 66–67. *See also* compact, statesmanship, and the right of revolution, Jaffa's defense of

Social Contract, 106

Socrates, 2, 84, 169

South Carolina Nullification Crisis, 61

"squatter sovereignty," 141

statesmanship. *See* compact, statesmanship, and the right of revolution, Jaffa's defense of

states' rights, Calhoun's argument for constitutionality of, 68

Story of a Soldier's Life, The, 23

Strauss, Leo, 4, 15, 39; Anastaplo as student of, 135; crisis of historicism asserted by, 43; democracy as aristocracy explained by, 105; Jefferson and, 109; Jefferson on natural *aristoi* cited by, 37–39; last book of, 108; Lincoln's voice adopted by, 26; most important statement made by, 106; "political philosophy" as queen of social sciences demonstrated by, 50; questions never answered by, 25; reference to American constitutional system by, 107–8; Zuckert's credit to, 26–27

"Straussian orthodoxy," 48

Summary View of the Right of British America (1774), 67

Taney, Roger, 120; denial of, 88; Lincoln's refutation of argument by, 142–43; Lincoln's ridicule of statement by, 83; matter of special concern for (in *Dred Scott* case), 75–76; portrayal of in House Divided Speech, 88; today's endorsement of view of, 146

Temperance Address (Lincoln), 98

Thayer's Greek-English